P9-CCI-079

NEW CAREERS
IN HOSPITALS

By

Lois Savitch Sigel

THE ROSEN PUBLISHING GROUP, Inc.
New York

Published in 1988, 1990 by The Rosen Publishing Group, Inc.
29 East 21st Street, New York, NY 10010

Revised Edition 1990

Library of Congress Cataloging-in-Publication Data

Sigel, Lois S.
    New careers in hospitals.
    Includes index.
    Summary: Discusses a variety of hospital careers, including health education, infection control, patient advocacy, and safety engineering.
    1. Hospitals — Vocational guidance — Juvenile literature [1. Hospitals — Vocational guidance. 2. Occupations. 3. Vocational guidance] I. Title.
    RA972.5.S58 1988   362.1'1'023   88-26467
    ISBN 0-8239-1172-1

Manufactured in the United States of America

Contents

Acknowledgments

I wish to acknowledge the special contributions of the Public Affairs Department, Allen B. Chackman (Safety and Education Coordinator) and Chris Viteo (Risk Management Coordinator) of the Medical College of Philadelphia, Pennsylvania I am grateful also to the institution for providing several of the photographs in the book, taken by Edmund Murray for various College publications.

I extend my sincere appreciation to the many supportive professionals working in Chicago and Philadelphia hospitals and health organizations who provide information and offered helpful suggestions regarding the writing of this book. Their interest made the development of the book a gratifying experience for the author.

A special thank you to Monica Dent who gave graciously both her time and computer expertise.

About the Author

Lois Savitch Sigel is a writer and is currently working as a health care consultant with a concentration in women's health programs. She received bachelor's and master's degrees at the University of Pennsylvania and later completed substantial work toward a doctorate in urban/health planning at that institution.

Before returning to Philadelphia, where she currently resides, Ms. Sigel lived in Chicago and worked as a hospital administrator at the University of Illinois Hospital performing several roles and assuming special responsibility for the patient advocacy program. Prior to assuming that position, she served on the faculty and as Director of the Internship and Career Programs at the School of Public Health. While at the University, she was active in the Senate and in several women's health projects, school curriculum development, and many hospital and campuswide committees.

Before going to the University, Ms. Sigel worked as a health manpower specialist in the Chicago regional office of the Public Health Service, where she evaluated grant proposals and managed the review process in the health professions education division. Prior to her move to Chicago she lived in Philadelphia, where she served as a manpower specialist in the Philadelphia regional office and as a consultant to several substance abuse manpower training projects developed and presented at the Eastern Pennsylvania Psychiatric Institute. She began her career in public health as a research associate in health manpower planning and education in the Department of Community Medicine at the University of Pennsylvania.

Ms. Sigel has been active in city, state, and national organizations, serving frequently as a chairperson or a member of planning committees for health systems agencies, the American Cancer Society, the American Nursing Association, the Association of Schools of Public Health, the American Public Health Association, and many other professional groups. She was the founder of the Career Center for the Illinois Public Health Association and an officer of the Illinois Chapter of the National Society of Patient Representatives. Recently she served on the Health and Ethics Committee of the Pennsylvania Humanities Council in Philadelphia.

Ms. Sigel is the author of numerous articles on public health and health manpower topics and a book on public health. She is married to a surgeon and has five children: Paul, Gwynne, Ellen, Adam, and Carin, who is married to Michael Schlesinger. This book is dedicated to her husband, Bernard, and their family.

Introduction

The hospital is an exciting place to work. A sense of drama is always associated with treating seriously ill people. And now, more than ever before, *only* patients who are very sick are in the hospital.

Because of government and health insurer regulations designed to contain the costs of medical care, doctors can hospitalize patients only as long as is absolutely necessary. They may not have patients admitted to the hospital without regard for the new regulations. As recently as a decade ago, physicians determined who would be hospitalized and made the decisions regarding length of stay for their patients. Now the length of stay is regulated strictly, and patients who are not sick enough to require an acute-care hospital must be treated in an outpatient facility. Others who are sick but cannot be improved significantly by hospital care must also be treated outside the hospital: through community programs, long-term care facilities, hospices, or other modalities.

Shortened stays and fewer patients eligible for admission to acute-care facilities are phenomena with broad and dramatic implications for the health care delivery system in the United States. The resultant changing role of the hospital is discussed at greater length, particularly in the chapters on planning and quality assurance, where utilization and the maintainance of quality care emerge as issues central to the viability of hospitals.

Some factors need to be noted in relation to the cost-of-care crisis. In the 1970s and early 1980s, the concept of *patient mix* became a serious concern of hospital administrators. Essentially, the growth in numbers of patients without health insurance or with lower-reimbursed Medicaid or Medicare coverage contributed to hospital deficits nationwide. To compensate for the lack of or limited reimbursement, hospitals needed to have more patients with private insurance. The private patients, in essence, helped pay the costs of free care. Services and procedures for most private care were reimbursed at cost or better: Insurers paid hospitals the amount charged for treatment. It became essential for hospitals to have a patient mix that would enable them to meet their budget demands.

Changes in the reimbursement policies of the public and the private insurers have rendered the balanced patient mix solution much less effective. The introduction of Diagnostic Related Groups (DRGs) in the early to mid-1980s limited the amounts that hospitals could be paid for some 400 kinds of diagnoses and procedures received by Medicare patients, no matter how much these services cost the hospital to provide.

Further, fixed-price systems in the private sector have emerged in the form of health maintenance organizations (HMOs) and preferred provider organizations (PPO) systems. These insurers have fixed-price reimbursement policies that force hospitals to provide services for patients at lower charges. In an effort to maintain favorable occupancy rates (required for accreditation), hospitals negotiate contracts with managed-care providers (one way to classify the fixed-price private insurers), often performing services for these patients at a loss to the hospital. In the last few years managed-care organizations have become extremely popular, increasing their membership significantly.

More inpatient care, therefore, is reimbursed below cost. Hospitals are pressured to close the gap between fixed-price reimbursement and the actual cost of providing services, because so many of their patients belong the HMOs and PPOs. Closing this gap is not an easy task, particularly with rising costs and fewer patients.

Hospitals now have a sicker patient population and receive less money to care for them. The change from cost-based to fixed-price reimbursement accelerated at a time when medical technology, personnel, and all kinds of maintenance costs were spiraling. The financial crisis and the sicker patient population are changing the hospital environment dramatically.

The work pace has been accelerated. Because the patients are so sick there is more work to be done, and, with staff reduced to cut costs, fewer personnel are available to perform all the functions. Staff must do more work in less time.

The drama that has always been associated with the hospital environment is heightened: The serious condition of most patients, shortened stays, and personnel overloads have elicited more negative reactions from staff, patients, and their families. The hospital is alive with activity twenty-four hours a day, seven days a week, every day of the year. Staff on day and night shifts are focused on the care of the acutely ill. They must be able to provide high-quality care in less time as well as respond with empathy to patients, their families, and friends. Patient representatives and risk management personnel hear constant threats of litigation from dissatisfied patients and relatives, whose complaints are frequently irrational in response to this frenetic ambience. You will read about the functions of patient representatives (or advocates) and risk management employees in this book and will see how their roles are affected by the changing hospital environment.

The hospital is a large and complex organization, much like a city unto itself, that depends on the effective performance of many different functions to serve its population adequately. In addition to treating patients for their illnesses, the hospital staff must provide food for them, see that their rooms are sanitary, ensure their safety by preventing fires, control infections in and eliminate toxic substances from their environment. These activities represent only a few of the total service requirements in the acute care hospital of today, where performance must meet heightened governmental standards and public expectations at a time when patients are sicker and funds are limited.

All kinds of clinical and support staff interact, working now at a faster pace to admit and discharge patients without delays, fixing faulty equipment that might be life-threatening if it is not repaired, distributing meals to patients in a timely fashion, performing all the many different tasks necessary to achieving the main goal of effective, efficient, and empathetic patient care.

Consumer expectations are higher, even though costs are making it more difficult to maintain even the traditional standards. Staff must make hospital stays as pleasant and comfortable as possible. Higher priority is placed on making information available to patients, providing comfortable areas for visitors, and offering other amenities that encourage the patient's communication with physicians as well as supportive interaction with family and friends.

Increasingly, the health care crisis stimulates hospitals to highly visible competition for *market share*: That means that they try to fill their beds by attracting as many patients as possible in a climate where there are fewer patients to be hospitalized. The higher priority on providing the amenities is, for the most part, the result of this competition. The amenities of patient care have become important for wooing a greater share of the market even though provision of routine quality care has become a challenge in this new environment.

Hospitals are providing special kinds of services in response to the public's demand for comfort and convenience. Many offer attractive housing for outpatients and visiting relatives close to the hospital. Others provide valet parking, daily delivery of newspapers and magazines, and suite accommodations for inpatients who are willing and able to pay for this luxury. The list of special amenities lengthens as the competitive spirit increases in the hospital community.

Sustaining quality care and making the hospital a more attractive environment become especially challenging as costs of maintaining the modern hospital, replete with current technology and other resources, continue to spiral. The 1990s will begin as a decade of crisis for the health care system unlike any it has faced in the past.

Many kinds of personnel work in the hospital to provide the new and traditional services intrinsic to the hospital experience. Groups of personnel, each with unique expertise, work together to provide quality care and service for patients. It is in the cooperative spirit of working together that hospital personnel realize one of the most valuable rewards of their professional lives. That may be one of the attractive features for you as you think about your future and the pluses that various careers can offer.

Physicians, nurses, physical therapists, occupational therapy specialists, physician's assistants, and other care providers depend on the contributions of nonclinical hospital personnel to perform their roles effectively. There are many of these workers, who complement the efforts of the clinicians. Departments in most hospitals include: housekeeping, safety management, dietary or food services, volunteers, risk management, legal services, admission and preadmission, public relations and marketing, health education, patient information systems, financial management, patient representatives, infection control, quality assurance, personnel or human resources, materials management, and purchasing. Larger hospitals often contain an even larger array of units that support the clinical activity.

Relatively new to the list are the departments discussed in this book. Many of them were performed prior to the last ten or fifteen years although they were not a major part of an administrator's or staff person's responsibility, nor did they play a discrete role.

For example, some of the activities of the public relations staff in a modern hospital used to be provided by nurses and other personnel if and when they had the time. Usually these workers had no special training in public relations skills such as writing or public speaking and were often expected, on short notice, to provide tours of the hospital and verbal presentations to visiting celebrities or reporters.

Public relations and marketing efforts have been increased substantially in the last few years, rising in priority to the top of the hospital administrator's list. Public relations and marketing directors (or vice presidents) work with the highest levels of management and are key to the planning and administration process. Professionals are highly trained and familiar with the national and political scene, marketing research, promotion strategies, and all areas of publication production.

During the 1980s certain functions became key to the effectiveness—often the survival—of the modern hospital. Primarily these are related to planning and image promotion and sustaining the quality of care in spite of declining financial resources. Special emphasis is placed on those activities that are particularly relevant to new mandates from regulatory agencies and insurers, such as quality assurance and safety management.

This book discusses the careers that were born out of the need to meet the new priorities. The activities associated with them existed before the 1980s but, like public relations, did not achieve their current status until the dramatic changes in the health care delivery system.

Major functions associated with each of the new roles are described. Regular duties assumed by departmental management have not been listed, since they are quite similar and can be mentioned briefly now. Only those administrative functions and the activities unique to the individual careers have been included in the appropriate chapters. General management responsibilities merit discussion in this introduction.

Administrative responsibilities of departmental directors or coordinators include planning, preparation, and general management of the budget. Budget planning and management is critical to the function of departmental administrators, especially during this period of waning financial resources. They must have a clear understanding of their department's goals. so that they can be consistent in their financial planning.

Administrators must communicate with and train personnel. They must be aware of individual shortcomings, abilities, and deficiencies so that they can allocate activities appropriately. When necessary they must plan, implement, and present training programs so that staff can function more effectively. Administrators must be sensitive to the professional and personal needs of their employees and know when to encourage and to counsel them so that workers are not only effective but also satisfied with their own work.

Good department administrators make sure that their staff is knowledgeable about hospital policy and changes in procedures and leadership. Often employees become preoccupied with their own work and oblivious to major happenings in the hospital that influence their professional roles. Department administrators must bring information to their staff regularly so that they are aware of its relevance to their work and can share the enthusiasm and the concerns of management and other employees.

Sharing of information is usually accomplished through departmental meetings or sessions with small groups of employees (if it is a large department) that focus on special issues and concerns. Directors schedule these meetings, plan the agenda, and usually preside at them. Not to be overlooked as an information-sharing opportunity is the everyday communication between department directors and employees. Informal interaction is critical to the morale of employees, particularly when administrators seek input for departmental decision-making. Often, greater rapport between administrator and staff is achieved through one-to-one interviews.

Department administrators are members and often chairpersons of hospital committees. They represent the interests of their unit in the larger group and they take back information to their employees.

As members of the senior administrative staff of the hospital, department administrators provide input into major decision-making by attending administrative conferences and workshops. They often represent the hospital at community conferences and bring back information to share with other members of the administrative staff and their own employees.

These, then, are the major administrative functions performed by department directors or coordinators. As the new occupations are discussed, other special management functions are described in the context of the scope of activities of each career.

If you are interested in working in a hospital and find satisfaction in meeting the new challenges in health care, one of these careers may be the rewarding profession that you are seeking.

Chapter **1**

Health Education

We all want to know more about our bodies and how to stay healthy. Each of us has a role to play in protecting our health. Physicians and other health providers acknowledge that it is practical to teach patients more about self-care so that they can help prevent disease and contribute to the healing process. Although physicians and other health care providers usually take charge of treatment when people get sick, they realize that what the patient knows about his health and his ability to use the knowledge are valuable tools that help speed recovery and prevent future illness.

The relationship between what we know and how it affects our health has increased efforts by care providers and various organizations to provide more health education for the public. Programs are available for those with acute and chronic illnesses as well as for persons who are well and want to know more about how to prevent disease. Health educators work with the intellectual, social, and behavioral factors that increase the ability to make informed decisions affecting personal health and the well-being of the community.

Many kinds of organizations provide resources for educating the public about health. Voluntary health agencies, groups established in response to needs for knowledge or services in special problems, usually have public information departments. They provide education through workshops, information hotlines, counseling, and referral services. The American Cancer Society, Planned Parenthood, and the American Diabetes Association are a few of the voluntary agencies that provide educational programs.

Health professional associations, organizations that represent their membership, provide information and materials for their members who present health education programs for the public. The American Medical Association and the American Public Health Association are examples of such professional associations. Voluntary agencies and professional associations are among the most active groups in providing health education opportunities.

Family doctors and other health care providers are important sources of health education for their patients. They counsel patients regarding acute and chronic problems and sometimes offer disease prevention recommendations. Colleges and universities, state and local health departments, and health maintenance organizations provide health education opportunities tailored to the populations that they serve. Many colleges, for example, operate physical fitness programs for students. Health departments offer well child care classes for new mothers and a broad range of other services, depending on the size of the department and the needs of its population. Health maintenance organizations provide nutritional and other health educational programs and hotlines for their members. High schools often provide special programs to prevent or abate drug abuse or to educate teenagers about birth control. Many large corporations have active employee benefits programs that offer workshops on how to stop smoking, control weight, and deal with stress. Substance abuse prevention and cessation programs are also popular at many worksites with a view to increasing productivity of workers who are at risk or are already addicted to drugs.

Background

In the past, most health education activity in hospitals was conducted by physicians as part of routine counseling of patients on a one-to-one basis. For instance, physicians instructed diabetic patients about diet, exercise, and use of their medication. They answered patients' questions about side effects of medicines or special problems associated with their disease. Sometimes doctors authorized nurses who worked closely with diabetic patients to provide routine counseling, saving the physician's time for specific problems or concerns of individual patients. Such one-to-one patient education persists in many doctors' offices, but other kinds of health education resources have emerged to supplement it.

Recently, health care professionals have recognized that patient education could be substantially improved if it were more structured, if it were planned, coordinated, and evaluated. This new approach is not meant to be a substitute for the one-to-one counseling that is part of the interaction between physician and patient. However, the planned courses have proven to be effective supplements, particularly in disseminating certain kinds of general information. Heart surgeons, for example, often recommend that their patients attend regular programs of diet and exercise instruction. They themselves continue to counsel patients during office visits, answering questions and making recommendations relevant to the individual condition. Health education using the group approach includes programs for patients with diabetes, heart disease, and high blood pressure. Prenatal care courses for expectant mothers and courses for patients who have had open-heart surgery are also popular.

In addition to one-to-one and group patient education, many hospitals have undertaken another kind of effort, usually described as health promotion. They provide services designed to increase awareness of the kinds of behavior that help prevent disease. These programs expand the role of hospitals, allowing them to reach out to the well population in the community.

Health promotion programs include health fairs, which provide disease-screening services, and health information sessions and materials for community members. They also include presentations or special workshops on such topics as good nutrition and how to build physical fitness. These services are usually free or available at minimal cost to consumers. Some hospitals have developed health promotion programs for workers in industry, and often these courses are presented at the worksites. Absenteeism is a major concern of most employers. They hire hospital staff to screen and provide educational programs for employees to keep them working more days of the year and thus enhance productivity. A typical program might include regular screening for high blood pressure; educational workshops that encourage good nutritional habits such as restricting the intake of salt and fried foods; and courses on controlling stress to prevent and treat high blood pressure.

Both patient education and health promotion in hospitals have increased substantially during the last fifteen years. In 1972 only 15 percent of hospitals surveyed had health education programs.[1] By 1978 the rate had increased to 62 percent. According to the same study, there had been a 65 percent increase in health education coordinating departments between 1975 and 1978, suggesting the growing importance of education in the hospital setting.[2]

Hospitals surveyed for a 1979 study indicated that more than 1,200 hospitals provided health promotion programs for business and industry and that many of these were presented at the worksite. Fifty-six percent of hospitals reported that they provided risk factor screening services to employees of local companies, and 35 percent had health education courses. Typically, the latter were workshops for substance abusers and heavy smokers.[3] Other kinds of programs are emerging: Healthful eating, fitness, and stress reduction are among courses that are becoming more popular. A recent survey (1985) showed that health promotion programs in hospitals almost tripled in six years: 3,253 hospitals (51 percent of responders) indicated that they had health promotion programs.[4]

As we shall see, the substantial increase and diversification in educational efforts during the last fifteen years has had an impact on the numbers and types of workers who provide health education in the hospital.

Professional Preparation

Because so many kinds of health education programs are provided by various departments in the hospital, several types of professionals function as health educators. Physicians, nurses, physical therapists, occupational therapists, and nutritionists or dietitians are among the health care providers who give one-to-one patient education as well as group courses and workshops. Many hospitals now employ personnel who have been trained as health educators in college and graduate programs, and they increasingly serve as leaders in the hospital's health education effort. Health promotion programs often are directed by health educators, usually working as part of a team that includes exercise specialists, nutritionists, alcoholic counselors, and other experts. Some hospitals coordinate all health education activities through one unit, usually in nursing or in a health education department. But the director or coordinator works with all the health professionals who contribute to the total program. For example, a director of health education at a community hospital might offer a workshop for industry personnel that features information and behavior modification techniques on substance abuse control. He or she might be a health educator with a college or graduate degree in the field but with little experience in the substance abuse area. The director could recruit a medical social worker employed by the hospital who has special training in substance abuse and regularly counsels patients. Together they would develop a course that might be presented by the social worker.

The health education director works with a nurse who runs the high blood pressure screening and information clinic. He or she works with the psychiatrist or psychiatric social worker who presents a stress control course to patients or to industry executives in high-tension positions. The director might even train and provide supervision for a hospital volunteer who presents newborn care sessions for teenage mothers. As you can see, health educators in hospitals represent a broad diversity of professional backgrounds.

Several kinds of college and university programs offer formal credentials in health education. Some are offered through departments of health education; others constitute tracks within departments. School health education is a department popular at many colleges. Schools and colleges of education sometimes offer degrees in health education. Many baccalaureate programs in nursing colleges offer health education specialties or coursework. Schools of Public Health or Colleges of Education have graduate programs for students interested in continuing their formal education in the field.

Most programs at the undergraduate level include courses in the biological, social, and behavioral sciences, educational methods, program organization and management, and field experience in organizations that provide health education. Emphasis is on oral and written communication skills and matching teaching methods with student populations and content areas. Graduate programs include these courses as well as courses in epidemiology and biostatistics, particularly useful in the development of evaluation skills.

Persons interested in careers in health education in hospitals must be open to on-the-job learning about new content areas, teaching formats, and working cooperatively with diverse health professionals. The scope of programs is broad and constantly expanding. Frequently, a health educator must develop and present a course in a content area in which he or she has little experience, because no other qualified professional is available. No formal educational program, in itself, could orient students to all of the areas of expertise that might be required. Willingness and the ability to adapt and learn on the job are critical to the effectiveness of persons working as hospital health educators.

Functions

Since the activities labeled as health education are so diverse in the hospital, the functions that professionals perform are numerous depending on staff assistance and many other factors. Counseling of patients and their families is ongoing, both in cooperation with health care providers and without their involvement. An educator may work closely with a pediatric surgeon, advising parents about the postoperative care of their child. Counseling also might include bedside talks with new mothers about their postnatal care, with the educator assuming total responsibility for determining the content of these sessions.

Hospital health educators design and teach courses as well as providing assistance to others who present courses and workshops. They prepare pamphlets and course materials when these are not available, which means that they research topics and write the material. Sometimes they are responsible for producing the course materials, necessitating the coordination of their work with photographers, printers, and others. They often must monitor the costs of the project to conform with budget allocations.

The evaluation of educational programs has become a priority of administrators in recent years, and health educators are expected to develop methods and tools for assessing the impact of programs. Effective evaluation includes knowing what questions to ask and how to ask them and being familiar with the statistical methods necessary to interpret the findings. The degree of statistical knowledge needed depends on the expertise in this area that is available. If they work at a university hospital it is probable that they can consult with statisticians employed by the university. In hospitals without statistical expertise, health educators would need more statistical skills. Future budget allocations for health education often depend on effective evaluation that demonstrates the

COURTESY MCP, EDMUND MURRAY PHOTO

Health education fair at a hospital.

utility of programs; thus professionals must be able to develop evaluation components for their projects.

Health educators may also have to market their programs since many hospitals, particularly small ones, cannot afford staff to focus on this function. Marketing entails researching the need for certain kinds of courses and determining where and to whom they should be offered. It also involves the preparation of written materials and sometimes the presentation of talks to potential users. Marketing requires some knowledge of the costs of various promotional strategies and materials and which are most effective for particular programs. For example, television commercials are expensive and may be no more effective than ads in community newspapers in promoting certain kinds of educational programs.

Health educators who coordinate hospitalwide educational activity must perform a major management function besides the usual responsibilities of an administrator, as discussed earlier. They often must supervise and coordinate the work of employees from other departments in addition to their own staff. Health education directors must work effectively with professionals from many disciplines, providing leadership without limiting autonomy. Maintaining good rapport with the cooperating professionals is a challenge that must be met. Persons interested in careers in this field must be aware of this challenge and have the interpersonal skills necessary to promote enthusiasm among all who participate.

Hospitals are fast-paced, dynamic, and exciting places to work. Anyone interested in health education who welcomes the diversity of an expanding role should consider employment opportunities in hospitals.

Salary

Persons who seek entry-level positions as health educators can expect a starting salary of $20,000 to $26,000, depending on level of education and experience. Those who direct departments of health education in hospitals can expect salaries ranging from $30,000 to $36,000, depending on their credentials as well as the size and previous activity of the department. Hospitals in rural communities usually pay less, and smaller hospitals offer lower salaries than large hospitals.

Because of the diversity of professionals who provide educational programs in hospitals, however, salary levels vary considerably and depend to a large extent on the professional discipline of the educator. Nurses in most states are well paid in entry-level positions; if they assume administrative positions and perform health education services as well, they can earn higher salaries than other educators even if they receive only institutionwide annual pay increases.

Job Outlook

Because disease prevention and self-care have become more acceptable to providers, it is probable that educational programs in all kinds of health care facilities will increase during the next decade. During recent years substantial numbers of physicians and other clinical professionals have realized the potential of education for decreasing their work load while effecting increased observance of good health habits. Health maintenance organizations, ambulatory care programs, community health centers, and primary care health centers are promoting health education for their populations. Several trends suggest that hospitals will become equally active in this area.

Recently initiated reimbursement policies of the public (Medicare and Medicaid) and private (e.g., Blue Cross/Blue Shield) health insurers discourage hospitalization for many ailments that can be treated on an outpatient basis. Utilization of new methods and technology has made it possible for many illnesses to be treated in the doctor's office or in a clinic. For instance, the use of lasers for cataract operations has made possible the outpatient treatment of a problem that used to require hospitalization. When a hospital stay is necessary, new insurer policies dictate that it be as short as possible. Medicare specifies the length of time that a patient can be hospitalized for treatment of a particular health problem. The hospital is reimbursed only for that time and care. Other insurers are moving in this direction, limiting hospital stays significantly.

Health education is a useful tool for providers who want to increase the patient's capacity for self-care to compensate for some of the limitations on hospital services. If you are interested in health education in the hospital setting, you should be aware of the many kinds of programs that will be needed because of this shift in emphasis. Read journals that discuss the latest trends in health care delivery, such as *Hospitals* and *Modern Health Care.* Knowledge about the shift to ambulatory care and the justification for more and different kinds of health education will be useful background for your job interview. It will also serve you well in planning health education programs after you get the job.

References

[1] American Hospital Association, AHA research capsules. *Hospitals* 1972, 46:102.

[2] American Hospital Association, Hospital Inpatient Education: Survey Findings and Analysis, 1978. Bureau of Health Education, Centers for Disease Control, Atlanta, 1980.

[3] Longe, Mary. "What's Going On in This Community?" *Hospitals* 53:171, September 16, 1979.

[4] AHA Hospital Statistics, 1986 Edition, Chicago, Illinois.

Chapter II

Infection Control

Most of us live and work in environments filled with bacteria and viruses, microorganisms that we call germs. We are surrounded by family members and friends who have illnesses caused by germs such as chicken pox, measles, gastritis, and the common cold, and we are at risk of contracting these when we are exposed to them. Since these are not serious illnesses, the situation poses no threat except to persons having certain chronic diseases with the potential for serious complications if they contract one of these minor diseases.

In some cases it is even considered desirable to catch these illnesses. Parents, for example, may want to expose children to chicken pox so that they will become immune and not risk getting the disease later in life when it could be more harmful.

Many other microorganisms in the environment are harmless and even beneficial. We take no precautions to protect ourselves from them. They often maintain the balance in the environment that scientists say protects us from deadly infections such as the influenzas that become international epidemics.

In most parts of the world good personal hygiene is practiced: washing of hands, keeping eating utensils clean, and other similar habits that we learn as children. Even though we observe these habits, most of us at one time or another have colds, rashes, and other diseases that are categorized as infectious, capable of being transmitted from one person to another. Usually these are not caused by dangerous pathogens. They are short-lived and at worst cause temporary discomfort and inconvenience.

When people enter hospitals, however, infections and their

sources become a real concern. Patients have contact with new pathogens, many of which can be serious threats to health. In addition, when people become hospitalized patients they often are more vulnerable to infection because of recent surgery or a serious episode relating to a chronic illness. Also, the complications that can result from infection may be more serious threats that can retard or jeopardize the recovery process.

In summary, patients' increased exposure to new types of microorganisms, their greater susceptibility to disease, and the potential for serious complications make infection control in the hospital an important concern.

Background

Before the relationship between microorganisms and disease was established, death resulting from infectious disease was significant. As late as 1900 in the United States, for every 100,000 in the population 115 persons died from diarrhea and enteritis and 185 from tuberculosis.[1]

Most hospitals had high infection rates. Around 1860 a maternity hospital in Vienna attended by physicians and medical students had a much higher death rate from childbirth infections than did a nearby facility attended only by midwives. Investigation of these findings revealed that the difference was related to the performance of autopsies. Physicians and students at the maternity hospital performed autopsies regularly and did not thoroughly clean their hands before they delivered babies. Initiation of a requirement that all medical staff wash their hands with a strong germicidal solution resulted in a significant reduction in the maternal and infant death rate.

Both Louis Pasteur and Joseph Lister worked to improve hospital sanitary practices. Pasteur discovered that germs were associated with the absence of sanitation and that high temperatures were effective in killing them. Armed with Pasteur's findings, Lister introduced the sterilization of suture materials and surgical instruments to help prevent infection during surgery. Shimmelbusch, a prominent nineteenth-century surgeon, recommended isolation procedures to minimize the spread of infection among

hospitalized patients. In his insistence on isolating infected patients and using special precautions in handling items with which
they had contact, he made an important contribution to what
became known as the "aseptic approach to the prevention of
infection."
Florence Nightingale championed the importance of proper
ventilation and housekeeping among nursing and medical staff.
Her influence on nursing practice was important at a time when
sanitary procedures were helping to reduce the incidence of
infection.
Practice of aseptic precautions in hospitals became widely
accepted and succeeded in minimizing infection. With the advent
of antibiotics and sulfa drugs, however, preventive practices became relaxed, and by the mid-1970s certain types of infectious
disease had increased and elicited new concern in the health
community.
The renewed interest in prevention was sparked by a number of
factors. Because of the increased mobility of people, diseases that
had been eliminated in most parts of the world were spread by
travelers. Levels of required immunity had also declined. By 1972
smallpox vaccination for travelers between European countries
and the United States was no longer mandated. The relaxation of
immunization requirements was simultaneous with the substantial
increase in world travel, prompting renewed efforts in infectious
disease control. Early in the 1970s public health officials warned
that measles was out of control, that diphtheria had reached its
highest incidence in eight years, and that many poor urban areas
were at risk for polio epidemics because the residents had not been
immunized.
Also, many bacteria had become resistant to antibiotics. New,
stronger drugs were developed, which frequently were not toler-
ated by patients. The development of resistance to insecticides
became a problem, especially when substantial amounts were used
in agriculture for killing malaria-carrying mosquitoes. The progress of the malaria eradication program slowed considerably:
Cases reported in the United States rose from 62 in 1960 to 3,997
in 1970.[1]
Incidence of communicable disease in the community is always a

concern for hospital personnel focused on reducing infection rates in hospitals. But it became more important when requirements for decreasing the length of hospital stays made it imperative to minimize infections. One of the main contributors to longer hospital stays is persistent infections that prevent discharge of patients. The active search for more effective antibiotics has been accompanied by a return to emphasis on prevention during the last decade. This focus has been supported enthusiastically by the public health community including the Public Health Service of the Department of Health and Human Services. It has been endorsed by some of the most influential groups in the health community, including the American Hospital Association (AHA), the Joint Commission on the Accreditation of Hospitals (JCAH), and the American College of Surgeons. The AHA and the JCAH recommended that all hospitals appoint an infection control committee. The JCAH mandated recently that at least a half-time person be designated to assume responsibility for infection control activities as his or her exclusive function.

The rationale for the renewed focus on prevention evolved out of both humane and economic concerns. If infection could be prevented, much unnecessary pain, disability, and death could be eliminated. In the economic area social costs provided a strong incentive. In 1977 about 1.84 million patients developed infections that added at least three days to their hospital stay at a cost of $174 per day excluding physicians' fees, totaling more than $966 million annually.[2]

Professional Preparation

Personnel who work in hospital infection control programs often are nurses who have elected additional training to prepare themselves for the role. Frequently they are designated infection control nurse or nurse epidemiologist, suggesting that they have had special training in epidemiology, the study of how disease develops and spreads in human populations. Often nurses who have served as nursing administrators or staff assume responsibility for coordinating infection control, sometimes while continuing to serve part time in another role.

Other persons qualified to serve as infection control specialists are those with baccalaureate degrees in the biological sciences, especially if they have had some courses in statistics and epidemiology. If they have a master's degree in public health with a specialty emphasis in epidemiology, they are in an excellent competitive situation.

Some public health schools offer nondegree programs in such areas as epidemiology. The Association of Schools of Public Health, in Washington, D.C., can provide information on the availability of these programs and the courses offered at the various schools.

Persons with a special interest in the biological sciences will find that working in infection control is an interesting way to apply their knowledge. They need to be patient with other workers and adept at communicating information, because they must impress upon all personnel the importance of adherence to infection control standards.

Functions

The scope and kind of activities assumed by infection control personnel vary to some extent in different hospitals. Differences depend primarily on the number of staff dedicated to the function and the level of importance it is given. Performing all the functions recommended for the prevention, surveillance, and reporting of infectious disease is a demanding job. In large hospitals, particularly, it requires continuous and exacting efforts.

The hospital environment is always under the close scrutiny of infection control workers. Because of the rapid turnover of people, bringing with them new sources of possible contamination, surveillance and reporting are part of the daily routine.

No area of the hospital can be overlooked as a place where infections start and thrive. Inpatient units are especially important to monitor because the sick patients are particularly susceptible to infectious disease that can complicate their recovery.

A patient who has had a surgical procedure, for example, is seriously threatened by microorganisms that cause wound infections. Proper and timely healing of incisions is important. An

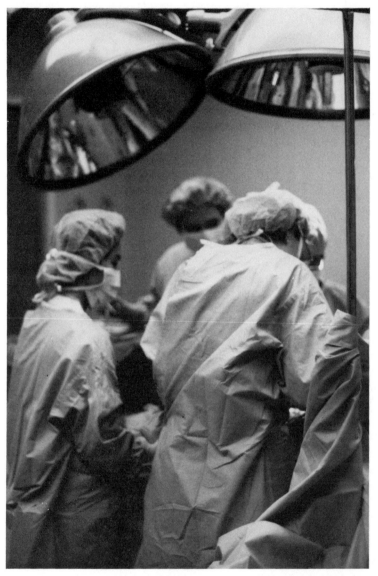

COURTESY DR. B. SIGEL

Infection control procedures are stringently observed in the operating room.

infected wound can influence the patient's recovery by causing additional discomfort and the development of other illnesses, thus increasing the length of hospitalization.

Infection control personnel usually make rounds in all inpatient units daily. Variations in the frequency of rounds depend on such factors as the number of personnel working in infection control and the level of risk to patients in a particular unit. Units that have persistent problems with infectious disease are monitored more frequently.

Personnel visit patients and talk with head nurses and other staff as they investigate infection problems in the various areas. They review records and charts, noting the presence of fever, skin rashes, and other indications of the presence of infection. They pay special attention to any changes in practice within the units, such as in the use of antibiotics, the frequency of patients in isolation, and the prevalence of soaking as a means of treating minor infections. Infection control personnel keep careful records of these changes in each unit. Early detection and eradication of infection can prevent many serious control problems in the hospital.

Maintaining good communication with the employee health service staff is part of the regular routine of infection control personnel. Because there are so many employees in a hospital and most of them have direct interaction with patients, they constitute a major risk for introducing and spreading disease. Careful monitoring of illness-related absences and treatment of minor infections also promote early detection and elimination of disease.

Infection control workers monitor laboratory findings daily, checking to determine what microorganisms are present in cultures taken from various patients. They visit the infected patients and monitor their progress carefully. The combination of regular surveillance of inpatient units and follow-up activity on laboratory reports constitutes much of the infection control effort.

Records of all infections that develop after a patient's admission are carefully maintained during his or her hospitalization so that the potential threat to recovery can be halted. Up-to-date records make it possible to determine appropriate action to minimize the impact of minor infections on the patient's health and on the quality of the hospital environment.

Workers also instruct and counsel individuals and groups of employees about procedures to prevent contamination. For example, if a nurse has a skin rash that is the result of infection or has an irritation that could become an infection, she might be advised to cover the area affected or to cease direct contact with patients until the rash disappears. Infection control personnel also check necropsy reports (records of patient autopsies) to find out if previously undiagnosed infection was found during autopsy. They establish a follow-up surveillance of discharged patients to elicit feedback on infections that surface after patients leave the hospital. The surveillance procedure must monitor all possible sources to promote early detection and minimize the spread of existing infection.

Very minor infections can become major problems in hospitals, especially those that house a large proportion of high-risk patients. Careful surveillance and reporting, as well as immediate action when indicated, is a responsibility that is assumed primarily by infection control staff but must be shared by all hospital employees.

The community surrounding the hospital must be evaluated regularly. If there is an outbreak of chicken pox or measles in the vicinity, for instance, infection control staff must know about it to initiate the proper precautions. They might decide to prohibit visits to patients by preschool and elementary school children, those most likely to be exposed directly to those diseases.

Infection control staff keep in contact with city, county, and state health departments to get information about community health problems. They talk to staff at local schools and other places where people congregate to learn about the incidence of disease in the neighborhood. Most hospitals have liberal visiting privileges except when there are local outbreaks of disease. Infection control staff must be aware of community health problems so that they can change visiting privileges and take other protective measures when they are warranted.

Infection control coordinators or directors perform special administrative functions in addition to the routine tasks discussed in connection with managing hospital departments. They participate actively in the infection control committee. Representatives of all the clinical specialties (e.g., pediatrics, surgery), hospital administration, nursing, and pathology meet regularly to develop infection control policies and procedures and systems to monitor their effectiveness.

Infection control managers work closely with the committee, sharing pertinent information with members and reviewing all infection control data with the committee chairperson weekly. They prepare monthly statistical reports and submit them to the committee and other personnel key to the promotion of the infection control program.

Salary

Persons who are registered nurses or have baccalaureate degrees in the biological sciences can expect to start working in infection control programs at a salary of $26,000 to $28,000. For persons with a master's degree or with substantial experience in the field, starting salaries range from $32,000 to $35,000, depending on such factors as the size and location of the hospital. Because many hospitals have half-time infection control coordinators who perform additional roles in the hospital , salaries can be influenced upward or downward depending on the pay scales of the other job.

Job Outlook

Because the spread of infection has become such a costly problem in the hospital, job opportunties are expected to increase as facilities, especially large ones, recognize the need for more personnel to ensure a comprehensive high-quality infection control program.

AIDS and other diseases that are spread internationally have created serious problems in hospitals. More infection control staff are needed to develop and implement protective measures. Because growing numbers of hospital employees are intimidated by the AIDS scare, new positions are created because of the extra workload and old ones become vacant because of increased attrition.

The establishment of effective infection control programs in hospitals has become key to the quality assurance effort that is a priority of regulatory agencies and health insurance payers. With this emphasis, career opportunities will be available for persons with the appropriate preparation and interest in this important work.

References

[1] Hanlon, John J. *Public Health Administration and Practice* (6th ed.). C. V. Mosby Company, Saint Louis, 1974.

[2] American Hospital Association Committee on Infection Control Within Hospitals. *Infection Control in the Hospital* (4th ed.). American Hospital Association, Chicago, 1979.

Chapter III

Marketing

The term marketing signifies all the activities associated with finding out what products and services consumers want from an organization and how to provide them. It includes determining what consumers do not want and reducing or eliminating those products. Marketing requires constant communication between sellers and buyers so that changes are made responsive to the buyers' needs. Finally, it culminates in the promotion of products to reach the consumers for whom they are targeted.

Marketing professionals must be willing to study consumers' needs in an objective way. They need to acknowledge that time and effort are required to learn what consumers think about their products and the constant changes that are made in response to market research findings. Marketing professionals must be willing to learn from their customers and recommend changes to reflect that input even when it conflicts with their own professional opinions.

The promotion of the product and subsequent changes in it also involve objective planning. Marketing personnel must be knowledgeable about all the ways to advertise their products, the costs of each, and the circumstances under which they are effective. Successful promotion is achieved when the population for which the product is intended is made aware of its value through the most cost-effective promotion available.

Marketing for hospitals is similar in most respects to that performed in most complex organizations. The focus of activities is on constant surveillance of the changes in the market potential of services and programs and how best to use available resources to promote them.

Personnel concentrate on the analysis and management of four factors basic to the delivery of health care. First is the product itself; for example, whether it is a diagnostic or therapeutic service and how it is intended to help patients. Will it make them live longer, or is its value more relevant to improving the quality of life by minimizing pain or increasing the ability to function in everyday life?

The second key factor is the setting of the program or service: where, when, and how it is delivered to the patient. Must it be offered in the hospital or can it be made available at an outpatient facility or in a doctor's office? Is the service available on a twenty-four-hour basis or only on certain days? Is it provided by technology or by counseling and education?

Of increasing importance to all personnel is the third factor, the price. That includes not only the charge for the service but all the other costs that contribute to what the patient must pay: admission and discharge of the patient from the hospital or outpatient facility, maintenance of the building in which the service is provided, and billing.

The fourth factor of special interest to marketing staff is promotion: how the patient becomes aware of and interested in using a product, word-of-mouth recommendations, and the overall process of publicizing it to current or potential users.[1]

All of these factors are crucial to both the selection of the user groups to which a service is targeted and the determination of the approach for promoting it. Marketing in hospitals, as throughout the health care industry, has become central to planning and management in this competitive consumer-driven market. Decision-making is dependent on determining which services sell and how they should be promoted. Administrators know the importance of the marketing function and have made it a top priority. Its status in the health care arena has generated many new employment opportunities.

Background

Ten years ago marketing of hospital services was one of those vague functions associated with public relations. It consisted of conducting occasional surveys of patients and neighborhood populations and advertising new programs and facilities. When a hospital opened a neonatal high-risk nursery, administrators hired a public relations firm to prepare ads for local newspapers, plan a promotional grand opening, and develop brochures and pamphlets for distribution to patients and visitors. The public relations staff person might have been assigned to assume these tasks, even though he or she had little training in the necessary skills. The scope of marketing and its importance as a function of hospital staff was extremely limited.

In contrast, developing and presenting a new health service in the 1980s is a much more elaborate and sophisticated process. A hospital planning a women's health center, for example, probably would survey potential users, analyze the data from questionnaires, and employ several other objective measures to determine if and in what form such a center would be salable. The administration might hire a professional research firm to work with the marketing staff on developing the necessary data to plan the project. The hospital's marketing personnel probably are trained in conducting consumer research as well as other aspects of the marketing function. But because marketing has become so specialized, it would not be unusual to use outside expertise for the research or any other aspect of the effort. Marketing staff would elicit input from the clinical faculty and key administrative staff, use the findings of the research consultants, and proceed through a defined process before deciding on the feasibility of developing a women's center and on the activities involved in promoting it.

The process would include sampling populations of potential users to determine precisely the most marketable form. Marketing personnel would need to know whether the center should be located in the hospital or in a small facility nearby, what hours it should be open, and what kind of staff it should employ.

Then marketing staff can review promotional strategies and select those perceived to be the most effective in attracting the targeted population. This, too, requires command of a body of specialized knowledge, and outside expertise may be used to work with hospital staff to determine the best ways to promote the center. Decisions need to be made on the advertising media to use: newspapers, television, radio, magazines, or a combination. The promotion plan must also include decisions regarding when to run ads and how they should look and sound. Marketing for hospitals has become a complex process that requires specialized staff working on a continuing basis, with or without the assistance of outside consultants.

As is evident from this brief comparison, the concept and scope of marketing in the hospital has changed significantly within the last decade. Once considered a routine function of minimal importance, it is now one of the highest priorities of hospital administration. Marketing has become central to the hospital's survival. Although the marketing of health services is perceived as a negative activity by its critics, the value to consumers can be considerable since it forces competition to provide high-quality services that meet the needs of consumers.

The rise of marketing to its current status in hospital management's priorities is attributable to many factors. Important among them are the rapid spiraling of costs of health care and the need to determine what services will compete successfully in the marketplace. Marketing contributes to cost containment by guiding the use of funds to ensure profitable returns on investments. If, for example, marketing research indicates that local industries are willing to pay for smoking cessation programs for their employees, then investment in hospital staff and materials for this effort is justified.

The increased need for cost accountability to consumers, government, and regulatory agencies gives special importance to the kinds of data collected in the marketing process. It is information that is often needed to justify the development of programs, building of facilities, and purchasing of equipment. Federal planning and other kinds of policy necessitate a constant supply of objective data to warrant expansion of all kinds of health resources, and marketing research provides this kind of information as part of its routine activity.

Marketing is important also because of its value as a resource for educating the public. Many promotional strategies make possible the dissemination of health care delivery information during the process of advertising a service or program. Education becomes a by-product of promotion. When, for instance, marketing staff promote the women's center, advertising materials that they prepare will discuss health problems and issues of special interest to women. Brochures and pamphlets will make potential users aware of services while also providing useful information for them.

Because consumers want to take an active role in decisions about their health care, they know that they need to acquire information. The information that promotional materials provide contributes to the pool of knowledge that they need for making sound decisions.

Marketing is also a means of increasing the sense of professionalism in the hospital. Nurses and other personnel receive high visibility as professionals when the programs and services to which they contribute are promoted. Capable administrators know the value of enhancing self-esteem and how it affects employee morale. Marketing affords the opportunity to reward staff.

Above all, marketing is critical in its promotional activity, which makes it possible for the hospital to highlight its programs and services so that it can compete successfully for its share of the patient market.

Professional Preparation

According to a recent survey of marketing personnel, 71 percent had bachelor's degrees in administration. About 8 percent had other undergraduate degrees. Among those surveyed, 68 percent had master's degrees also, but most (34 percent) were in fields other than business or hospital administration. Twenty-six percent did have master's degrees in business administration, and another 8 percent in hospital administration.[2] Although specific data on the "other" category of degrees cited is not available, discussions with professionals indicate that many have graduate degrees in public health, communication, journalism, and public relations.

When the survey was conducted, most of the marketing personnel in the sample had been in their positions for a short time: 50 percent for only one year, 20 percent for two or three years, 23 percent for four or five years, and 7 percent for five years or longer. They had backgrounds in marketing, public relations, planning, and a variety of other fields.[2] Those with previous experience in marketing often came from fields other than health and received some of their training in advertising agencies and public relations firms.

The short tenure of most of the personnel in their present positions is best explained by the sudden increase in employment opportunities during the early 1980s. Many hospitals employed no marketing personnel until recently and then increased their staff to four or five persons over a short time.

Functions

Marketing professionals who work in the hospital assume a broad scope of activities. Sometimes their role encompasses public relations and planning, and many administrative titles reflect responsibility for this combination. Even when marketing is designated as the single function of the department, there is considerable diversity in the activities required if management pursues a comprehensive approach.

As discussed earlier, the major goal of marketing is to determine what people want and how to promote those services and products. In the current market the effort is complicated by the diversity of needs of the groups for which services are targeted, contributing to an increase in the diversity of functions.

These user groups are composed primarily of patients, physicians, employers of sizable numbers of personnel, government and regulatory agencies, and employees of large organizations. Programs and services developed by hospitals have to meet the needs of all these groups, who often have conflicting priorities. For employers, the highest priority may be to keep insurance costs low, and hospitals that contribute to this goal by providing cost-effective services rate high with them. Employees, however, may be willing to pay more for health benefits if the services they need are easily accessible and provided in a comfortable environment. Marketing functions must reflect the needs of all these groups. Patients need consumer-oriented information, and marketing personnel must provide it in promotional materials. Efforts should be directed to the regular users of the hospital and to a broad population of potential patients who live in the neighborhood.

Physicians are important because they play a major role in managing care. To a large degree they control the flow of patients to inpatient and ambulatory care facilities. Marketing professionals must convince physicians that their patients will be satisfied with the services and programs offered. They must also teach physicians how to use the hospital cost-effectively. For instance, they need to provide information on use of outpatient surgery centers: what to tell patients about the advantages of these programs. Promotion of services to doctors must be tailored to meeting their needs, many of which are different from those of patients.

When employers in large organizations select insurance options for their employees, they also choose facilities. For example, health maintenance organizations (HMOs) as insurers contract with certain hospitals to serve consumers that they cover. If employers are not satisfied with the hospitals in an HMO system, they may choose not to offer that particular HMO to their employees. Marketing personnel must be aware of the preferences of employers and give them information that will show how the hospital meets their standards.

Government and regulatory agencies affect the actions of hospital management significantly, increasingly so as their numbers and powers expand. Marketing personnel must be able to supply them with the data they need so that they can approve the administration's choices of facilities, programs, and services, often determining whether or not the hospital can compete for its share of the market.

Finally, marketing staff must make their services more appealing than those of other hospitals competing for employees' patronage. Staff must be aware of the programs and special amenities offered by their competitors. Working mothers, for instance, may consider evening and Saturday visiting hours to be a necessity for the health care facility that they use. Marketing for these employees must emphasize the availabilty of this service and other amenities that have a high priority for certain users.

The employee group includes the hospital's own personnel. Support of the hospital is demonstrated most visibly by employees' use of the hospital for their own care. It indicates their confidence in the hospital's ability to provide high-quality and humane care, encourages high morale within the facility, and promotes a favorable image to other user groups.

The marketing effort must begin with the development of a profile that identifies weaknesses and strengths in programs and the extent of their appeal to the various user groups. Staff must consider which of the services need to be developed and which should be eliminated. Profile development includes exploring trends and examining why some programs are used and others are not. It is concerned with exploring the success of comparable programs at competing hospitals. It includes looking at the hospital's image as perceived by its patients and competitors. Professional staff throughout the hospital should provide input for the development of the profile. It can be described best as a "sketch of the hospital's system," and its accuracy will be enhanced by considering the hospital's image from many perspectives. A profile that reflects the hospital accurately can help to define the best approach for marketing efforts.

Developing the profile requires considerable research, a function key to all the other activities of professionals in the field. Research is an ongoing effort to determine who the users are, what they want, and how best to publicize the services to them. Marketing research personnel should know about the existing data, what they need to use, and where to find it. They should know how to design questionnaires and analyze the responses. They must know how to store the information and organize it so that it is easily accessible to them and others who use it. Marketing research includes use of all the possible methods of acquiring information, and professionals must be aware of and know how to utilize them effectively.

Research provides the information necessary for thoughtful decision-making about the choice of services and programs. Justification for expenses incurred in developing new services and programs needs to be based on findings of careful research and not the whims of administrators or clinical staff. Research is ongoing, since new data are constantly needed to evaluate the success of programs and make the necessary modifications.

The marketing research team must know what they are looking for and how to interpret their findings. For example, they should know what criteria to use to determine the worth of programs and services. They must know the difference between services that generate funds directly and those that attract users to other services in the hospital. An example of the latter are most emergency rooms and some satellite primary care centers, which may not generate substantial funds directly but are essential to bring patients into the hospital to use those services that do make money.

Research is also needed to know how to promote services to the various populations of users. Promotion is a major function of marketing professionals and involves a variety of specialized activities. It includes the promotion of new ideas among hospital staff so that change is more acceptable to them. They must also publicize new services and programs to employees so that they are familiar with the options and can discuss them with other workers, patients, and visitors. A knowledgeable staff is a valuable resource for marketing, demonstrating the high morale and pride of the organization.

Marketing staff may also work with personnel in individual departments to implement the changes that have been indicated by market research findings. They may help the director of admissions promote a new admission process intended to reduce waiting for patients. This would entail explaining the process and the research that led to the change.

The need to house relatives of hospitalized patients is becoming a concern for management, particularly when there are no reasonably priced hotels near the facility. Survey findings may confirm this concern, and marketing staff may be assigned to work with administration and other departments on implementing a plan to fill this need.

Many popular new services have been initiated in response to consumer input. They include programs for counseling adolescents, special self-help support groups, valet service for handicapped patients making visits to outpatient facilities, health promotion programs such as smoking cessation and substance abuse prevention, and special discharge planning and home health programs.

COURTESY MCP, EDMUND MURRAY PHOTO
Promoting the new Short Procedure Unit (day surgery).

The promotion of new services to the public involves a wide variety of distinct functions. Professionals must be knowledgeable about the hospital's user groups so that they can select the services appropriate to each. They need to know, for example, if their patient and employee populations contain sizable numbers of adolescents before they promote certain programs to either or both of these groups. If there are many teenagers in both groups, it is reasonable to develop and publicize programs such as family planning, adolescent counseling, and substance abuse prevention. One of the most important aspects of successful promotion is knowing as much as possible about the user groups so that services can be targeted to appropriate populations.

Marketing professionals need to know what methods to use to reach specific populations. They may want to use a different approach, for instance, to promote a service to teenagers in the patient group than to those who are part of the employee population. Workers are usually unavailable during the daytime; thus afternoon radio or television spots should not be aimed at them but might be appropriate for teenagers in the patient population. Marketing staff need to be skilled in choosing the most effective method for a given project and population.

They also prepare many of their own materials. They must learn to tailor their style to the population they are trying to reach. Employed teenagers are probably more sophisticated, so presentations for them should employ a different vocabulary than that in materials prepared for adolescent patients. Selecting the right services for individual populations, using appropriate methods, and adapting presentation styles for each are among the important functions performed in promoting services and programs in the hospital.

A recent survey of hospital administrators indicates which activities they perceive as most essential in marketing. Highest on the list are: conducting attitude surveys of current or discharged patients (100 percent); studying services offered by nearby hospitals (97 percent); presenting informational seminars for doctors (94 percent); making lounges available for doctors (88 percent); defining hospital target markets (89 percent); developing demographic profiles of patient populations (88 percent); and designing marketing research techniques to assist in feasibility studies (86 percent). Most of these functions are categorized best as marketing research, activities that are frequently neglected in actual practice. Results of the survey confirm this perception: Virtually all the administrators indicated that patient attitude surveys deserved high priority: only 70 percent actually carried them out in their hospitals.[3]

Marketing is a new and exciting career in the hospital. It is especially attractive to those who enjoy channeling their enthusiasm and creativity to reach out to patients and potential users of the hospital, discerning their needs, and designing promotional strategies for winning their favor.

Salary

Average annual incomes reported in a recent survey indicate that directors of marketing earn $43,525 and directors of planning and marketing make only $42,050. In contrast, persons titled vice president for planning and marketing receive salaries of $54,750. If the director of public relations also assumes the leadership position for marketing, he or she earns only $37,250.[1]* Titles appear to influence the salary level substantially, indicating the status of the marketing function, at what level it is managed, and thus, its place in the financial hierarchy.

Personnel working in the field say that salaries in general are higher that those of most other hospital workers with comparable education and experience. Most entry-level jobs pay in the middle to high $20,000s for persons with some marketing experience. Directors of marketing with a master's degree usually earn above $40,000, particularly those who work in hospitals in metropolitan areas.

Job Outlook

Because marketing now has a high priority in the health field, opportunities for entry-level and advanced positions are plentiful. Larger hospitals (those with 400 or more beds) have bigger staffs and probably already have departments to perform marketing (or marketing and/or planning and/or public relations) functions. Many opportunities for employment still exist in these facilities, but many smaller hospitals and those in suburban areas or small towns may offer more and better job choices because they have just begun to develop their marketing effort.

If you have little experience in the field, smaller hospitals might be more willing to accept your credentials. Gaining experience in

---

* The AHA cautions that these average income figures should be used for comparison purposes only, since actual salaries were not used to compute them. Respondents gave a "range," and those with incomes of $50,000 plus were designated as earning a maximum of $60,000 (even when they made more) for calculation purposes.

the field is important. Starting at a small hospital, perhaps in a suburban area, provides good experience for newcomers and makes them more competitive for openings. Working on health accounts for public relations firms, advertising agencies, and promotion departments of newpapers or magazines also serves to enhance credentials for marketing positions in hospitals.

Marketing is one of the most rapidly developing activities in the hospital. As noted, many hospitals now have vice presidents whose major responsibility is to oversee the function. Hospital administrators look for persons with leadership potential for the marketing team. Opportunities for advancement into senior management are good. Persons considering a career in health administration with ambitions for reaching a top administrative job are wise to consider entering the field in a hospital marketing position.

References

[1] Rowland, Howard S. and Beatrice L. *Hospital Administration Handbook*, Aspen Systems Corporation, Rockville, Maryland, 1984.
[2] AHA Society for Hospital Planning and Marketing, Summary of 1985 Membership Survey, American Hospital Association, Chicago, 1985.

Chapter IV

Patient Advocacy

Have you ever been a patient in a hospital? Or perhaps someone close to you—a parent, a sibling, or a good friend—has been hospitalized and you have been directly involved in his or her experience with the health care system. You may have been responsible for interacting between family members and health care providers or for giving the patient news about family and friends to minimize the sense of aloneness that most patients dread. Naturally, you wanted your friend or relative to feel as comfortable and secure as possible and were disappointed when less than sympathetic and competent care was provided.

Sometimes every effort is made to provide patients with special amenities as well as day-by-day reports on their condition. Whenever possible, special foods, magazines, and answers to health questions are provided. Too often, however, physicians and other providers of clinical care fail to respond to the emotional needs of patients. This can detract from the recovery process. If you or someone close to you has been denied the essential communication or the humanistic aspect of health care, this chapter will be of special interest to you.

Patient advocates, patient relations personnel, or patient representatives (the occupational title given by the American Hospital Association) are professionals who focus on the human touch in health care. They work to achieve effective communication between providers and patients. Recently, a colleague described what happened to a young woman who was raped at a subway station but was able to make her way to a hospital emergency room for help. The resident physician spent most of the time

COURTESY DR. B. SIGEL

A highly visible patient relations department close to the main entrance of the hospital.

during the examination reprimanding her for traveling alone on public transportation at night. The young woman, already traumatized by the assault, was so intimidated by the physician's comments that she was unable to provide a meaningful account for the medical record and police report. Acting on the advice of a nurse in the emergency room, she returned to the hospital early the next morning and consulted a patient representative. The patient rep helped her to modify her statement so that the report was accurate and more detailed and the police could act on the information.

Later, the patient rep spoke with the emergency room physician and explained the importance of the physician's support for victims of violence. She explained to the doctor that he is one of the first human contacts for such traumatized persons, and his or her behavior can have a profound influence on the victim's emotional resiliency, especially during the first few hours after an assault. By discussing the doctor's behavior with him, the patient rep attempted to modify patient-physician interaction, contributing to the solution of similar problems that could arise in the future. It is important that patient reps do more than apply Band-aids to individual problems. They should attempt to influence long-range problem-solving.

Patient reps frequently work in a variety of ways to change the system so as to prevent future mishaps. They report problems that they encounter, often to the highest levels of administration, and make recommendations or changes in staffing or systems to prevent or minimize recurrences. For instance, the patient rep in the above situation reported the case to the director of the hospital and suggested a plan to assign trained staff to the emergency room to work with assault victims supportively as soon as they come in.

Special comforts and conveniences can dramatically affect a patient's hospital experience and, often, the actual recovery process. Patient reps try to provide services that individualize care and contribute the human touch to a hospital stay. By honoring requests for particular magazines, newspapers, or foods, by explaining the use of temperature controls and other mechanical devices in the rooms, and by offering friendly and upbeat conversation, the patient rep can personalize health care and minimize the threatening ambience of the hospital environment.

Background

Perhaps because of the growing and outspoken demand for humanistic health care, the number of patient representative programs has spiraled in the last fifteen years, from only five in 1970 to over 3,300 by 1986.[1] Various phenomena have contributed to this growth, including the frequency of negative experiences reported by health care consumers. The status of intervention on behalf of the consumer received a special boost in 1970, when the National Welfare Rights Organization criticized the American Hospital Association for the lack of consumer input in its Committee on Health Care for the Disadvantaged. The Committee subsequently modified its membership to include a one-third consumer representation and reviewed a lengthy list of patient concerns. A Patient's Bill of Rights, passed by the Committee in December 1971, was later modified and endorsed by the legal staff and the Committee on Physicians of the American Hospital Association. Final approval of this first Patient's Bill of Rights was confirmed by the AHA Board of Trustees in November 1972, representing a major step forward in promoting safety and personal dignity for all health care consumers.

The Bill of Rights asserts, in essence, that the hospital should support the protection of patients' rights as an integral part of the healing process. The rights noted include considerate and respectful care, access to all relevant information on one's health status, and information for giving informed consent prior to receiving treatment. The Bill acknowledges the patient's option to elect any treatment recommended by health care providers with full understanding of the medical consequences of his decision. It further specifies the right to a clear explanation of the Bill. Patient handbooks and brochures distributed by hospitals now usually contain a summary of the Patient's Bill of Rights.

During the time when the Bill was being formulated, the federal government took action regarding patients' need for greater control of their medical care by initiating the Fry investigation. In 1971 the Secretary of the Department of Health, Education, and Welfare (now the Department of Health and Human Services) was directed to appoint and convene a commission to focus on the issue of medical malpractice. One of the first acts of the commission was to engage Fry Consultants, Inc., to make a study of patient grievance mechanisms in hospitals and other health care organizations. The main objectives were to review current procedures and programs and to make recommendations for change that would assist patients in eliciting satisfactory responses to their concerns.

The findings of the Fry study revealed considerable diversity in the backgrounds of patient advocates, the roles that they assumed, the types of complaints presented, and the work performed. Some of the advocates had college degrees and substantial experience in health care delivery; others had only high school diplomas and little or no exposure to the health field. Most program heads were men, and most were appointed by the chief executive officer of the organization.

According to the Fry study, complaints came from patients or their relatives. Only infrequently did nurses, physicians, administrators, or legal staff report incidents that infringed on patients' rights. The role of patient representatives consisted primarily of problem resolution or serving as mediator between patients and institutional personnel. It was unusual for them to suggest remedial action to the legal staff or to the chief executive officer of the hospital. The few patients who did ask for legal assistance were usually referred to the Legal Aid Society.

Most of the complaints reported in the study related to negative attitudes of nurses and physicians, hospital bills, insurance problems, poor housekeeping and dietary services, loss of valuables during hospitalization, faulty admission procedures, and emergency room delays. Many of these are still priority concerns of patient representatives.

The report cited the activities most common to patient grievance departments: (1) responding to complaints by visits to the patient, telephone calls, and written reports; (2) talking with patients and their families to obtain firsthand accounts of complaints; (3) investigating complaints by talking with involved professionals and other observers (few were allowed to examine patients' medical records); (4) making corrections in an effort to resolve problems; and (5) following up to see if problems had been remedied.

The models for patient grievance systems that were recommended by the Fry Report specified a much more active role for
patient representatives. Partly in response to this directive, visible
and assertive hospital programs have been developed during the
last decade. Each of the three models proposed in the Report called
for a thorough investigative process involving direct interaction
with all departments of the hospital, ongoing input at decision-
making forums, access to confidential documents as needed, and
proof that the solution met with the patient's satisfaction. When
that satisfaction was not possible because of misunderstandings or
errors by the patient, the rep was responsible for explaining in
detail to the patient, the family, or both why the complaint was
not justified.

The sixteen years since the publication of the Fry Report have
been significant for the development of the profession. Consumer
advocate positions have emerged in a wide variety of organizations
throughout the United States, from department stores to city and
state health departments. With the substantial increase in malpractice suits and the dissatisfaction expressed by more and more
health care consumers, the movement for programs in hospitals
has continued to gather momentum; from the relatively few investigated by the Fry Consultants, the number rose to 3,084 in 1982
and 3,305 in 1986.[12]

Evidence suggests that in spite of severe cutbacks in hospital
personnel, the fledgling patient rep profession is surviving and
making substantial gains in status. A National Society for Patient
Representatives was established within the AHA in 1972, and
state chapters quickly followed suit. Currently, about 60 percent of
all hospitals have patient rep programs and at least forty states
have professional society chapters.[1]

Professional Preparation

The educational level of patient representatives has risen
substantially since publication of the Fry Report. Nearly 60 percent of those responding to a recent AHA survey had baccalaurate
degrees; more than a third had master's degrees, and some had
additional graduate work beyond those degrees.[2] The type of edu-

cational background varies: Many come to the field with nursing and social work credentials, whereas others have preparation in the humanities and social sciences and gain their health care expertise by working in hospitals or other health care organizations. Findings of an earlier survey confirm that a sizable number (64.3 percent) had worked in other jobs in their hospital prior to their appointment as patient reps.[1]

Most professionals in the field agree that no one kind of educational preparation is best. They do feel, however, that a college degree is required and that familiarity with hospitals and outpatient care facilities is a must. To work in the field, it is important to become aware of the problems associated with receiving good and humanistic health care from the consumer's perspective. You need to learn about issues of costs and insurance reimbursement, the roles and training of clinical providers, and the communication gap between those who give care and those who receive it.

Since most patient reps are thirty-five years and older, according to the latest data, it would seem that quite a few have had substantial experience in health care before assuming their current positions.[2] The need for ongoing education in their area of expertise, however, is evidenced by the numbers of responders to the most recent survey (about 75 percent) who indicated that educational programs were one of the most important services offered by the National Society.[1] The best advice to those aspiring to positions in this field is to seek out and utilize all resources for learning about the areas covered by program assignments. As is shown by the functions described below, the breadth of roles now assumed by personnel in many of the hospital programs provides a challenge to those in search of competence in this field.

Functions

According to the Fry Report, most patient advocates in hospitals during the early 1970s limited their role to the resolution of patient problems. Only occasionally was there an opportunity to provide input for hospitalwide planning based on their experiences.

In contrast, patient reps currently assume responsibility for sharing their findings with senior staff on a regular basis. In many hospitals and outpatient facilities, patient questionnaires are distributed and interpreted by patient representatives, who develop reports that are shared directly with senior administrative staff. They participate in a wide variety of policy-making committees, especially those involved with ensuring patient/family comfort, the quality of care provided, and the ethical practice of medicine. They are also key members of committees charged with solving specific problems in areas such as patient admission and discharge. These committees often focus on promoting cost containment for the hospital. Patient representatives, while working to develop money-saving proposals, provide a balance in the decision-making process as they ensure that patients' rights are not sacrificed by cost-effective measures that are initiated.

The experiences of patient representatives are often shared with the highest levels of management. Program directors report directly to hospital management, in part so that they can keep the administration up-to-date on recurrent problems. In the 1986 survey about 82 percent of patient rep directors reported to the chief executive officer (director, executive director, or president) or the associate or assistant administrator of their institution.[2]

The focus today has shifted to inquiry/problem-solving (58 percent of programs), with the complaint/grievance responsibility as a second priority (36 percent). Third place (6 percent) is devoted to activities best described as personal and comfort services; e.g., seeing that specific amenities are provided for patients who request them.[1]

With the heightened emphasis on cost-effectiveness in hospitals, patient rep programs have significantly increased the scope of their responsibilities beyond these primary functions. According to the most recent survey of respondents, they are involved in a variety of areas separate from but related to their usual tasks.

Patient rep programs (38 percent) provide guest relations training, which means that they develop and run special programs to teach hospital employees how to relate more effectively to patients and their families, as well as their peers, so as to promote a cooperative and team approach. They are involved in certain risk management activities (21 percent) that focus on easing patients' anxieties when treatment problems occur and helping patients recover valuables lost during hospitalization. (More about these functions in Chapter VIII, Risk Management.) Volunteer service supervision (15 percent) is another activity currently assumed in patient rep programs, involving the responsibility for recruiting, training, and managing the volunteers in all parts of the hospital. Patient reps are also active in monitoring patient care through quality assurance activities (13 percent), checking that practices recommended for maintaining quality care are followed at all times. Some 4 percent do utilization review work (collecting information for accrediting organizations), and another 11 percent perform a variety of functions in which they serve as liaison personnel between physician staff and hospital administration.[2]

Sometimes these functions are assumed by other departments in the hospital, as is discussed in other chapters. But many patient reps have expanded their role to include these tasks, particularly in smaller facilities where two or more departments are combined, but even in larger ones where occupancy rates have fallen substantially and personnel cuts have necessitated increased work loads for remaining employees.

Interviews with professionals in the field indicate that patient reps have also been heavily involved in marketing and hospital-wide promotional activities. As discussed earlier, many hospitals did not have separate marketing divisions until the last few years. Consequently, other kinds of workers performed functions later assumed by marketing and development specialists.

In essence, since the publication of the Fry Report the patient representative role has emerged as one that interfaces with most units in the institution. These professionals plan for and promote a humanistic and individualistic aspect to patient care. They stress the importance of maintaining the dignity and comfort of the patient, in the planning of services as well as in patient interaction with all hospital personnel. In an era of burgeoning competition among hospitals, patient representatives could become key figures in providing the amenities that make one hospital more attractive than others to health care consumers.

Salary

Although salaries in the field are not high in comparison to many other hospital workers with similar educational levels, they have increased somewhat in recent years. According to recent surveys, about 55 percent made less than $20,000 in 1982.[1] By 1986 less than 22 percent indicated earnings at this low level.[2]

The generally low income level is probably related to the large number of women in the field: 92 percent of patient reps are women. As salaries of women health professionals rise generally, gains should begin to appear. To some extent, this phenomenon is reflected in the surveys. In the 1986 survey, about 79 percent of patient reps reported that they earned more than $20,000 per year, with more than 25 percent having salaries above $30,000 and 10 percent over $35,000.[2] These levels are higher than those reported in the 1982 survey.

Job Outlook

In spite of the cutbacks in overall hospital staffing during the last few years, patient representative programs have increased their staff (46 percent) or maintained the same number of personnel (43 percent).[2] With increased emphasis on competition and the role of consumers' input and satisfaction levels, more of these professionals will be needed to serve as liaison personnel, providing constant and insightful feedback that reflects the patient's perspective. If you derive satisfaction from working with people to help them solve their problems and want to contribute to improving the health care delivery process, you should explore a career in patient advocacy. Exciting challenges await you!

References

[1] American Hospital Association, National Society of Patient Representatives, Report of Membership Survey, February, 1982.

[2] American Hospital Association, National Society of Patient Representatives, Report of Membership Survey, February, 1986.

Chapter **V**

Planning

Planning for health care organizations is a complex process. It has become even more difficult in recent years when financial constraints, new reimbursement policies, and government regulations have to be considered before any decision is made. The "good idea" of administrators and key physician staff used to become reality in the hospital sometimes in a few months. This kind of planning and implementation is no longer possible because of the many restrictions within and external to the health care system. Administrators need to be knowledgeable about all the issues that influence decision-making. They must be able to maintain financial stability and the quality of patient care while they cope with day-to-day problems and plan for the future.

The hospital administrator must take the lead: organize and guide a formal planning process. First, he or she must select competent personnel to direct the planning effort: people who can stimulate effective planning in departments and coordinate those efforts with hospitalwide priorities. The administrator must know about the quality and types of services in the hospital and how they compare with those at competing hospitals. He or she must be able to identify program gaps and know how to develop and introduce those services if and when resources are available. The administrator must be aware of trends so that he or she can direct policy and strategy planning and monitor evaluation and follow-up activities rigorously to maintain a viable planning effort for the hospital.

Leadership by the administrator or chief executive officer (CEO) means providing direction for developing and maintaining a comprehensive planning program. Hospital planning involves working with architects and interior design specialists to build and equip new facilities and to remodel existing space. Planning means identifying the need for new services and recommending that others be reduced in size or eliminated when these actions are dictated. It includes monitoring the purchase of new equipment and helping to determine when new technologies represent cost-effective investments. Hospital planners also collect the information necessary for compliance with governmental and regulatory agencies' requests. They prepare CONs (certificate of need statements) for review by local and state planning agencies to justify requests for new equipment and facilities in conformity with government regulations. The scope of hospital planning is broad and varies depending on the priorities, resources, and level of comprehensiveness to which management is committed. Hospital planning involves the ability to make decisions based on available information, sometimes in abundance but in other instances quite limited. It challenges planners to make and implement these decisions in ways that are acceptable to hospital staff and the consumer population affected by the changes that result.

Background

Some program and facility planning has been ongoing in hospitals for many years. Federal and state legislation enacted between the 1940s and 1960s encouraged health organizations to be more active in their planning efforts. Some federal programs provided funds for hospitals to build new facilities and expand existing ones. (e.g., the Hill-Burton Act). Facility planning became popular, but it was usually directed by architects and consulting firms, who invited only limited input from hospital personnel. Planning in this era was intermittent, focusing on special projects such as building a new wing or remodeling the lobby.

Planning as an ongoing function performed by specialized professionals working in the hospital is a relatively new phenomenon. Not until the last decade, beginning with the implementation of Public Law 93–641 (the Health Planning and Resource Development Act of 1974), did hospital planning emerge as a distinct function carried out on a continuing basis. The 1974 Act established health care priorities to be developed and managed by a network of local and state health systems agencies. The agencies worked with hospitals and other health organizations to achieve their goals through the cost-effective planning of programs and facilities.

Many hospitals established planning programs in the late 1970s in response to the Act and its mandate. Administrators quickly became aware of the need for good information collecting and a variety of other planning functions so that they could respond to HSA (health systems agency) requests for well-prepared certificates of need enabling them to build new facilities and purchase equipment.

The focus of hospital planning evolved in three stages after the passage of the 1974 Act. The first emphasized facility planning, primarily the replacement and expansion of existing hospitals and outpatient facilities. The second stage concentrated on the introduction of strategic planning. During the early 1980s hospitals adopted a strategic business approach to developing programs and services. Strategic planning looks at the total hospital system and determines where monies will be spent relative to changes in the financial resources available in the hospital.

The change in focus to strategic planning came about largely as a result of what was occurring outside the hospital. During the 1980s health care organizations had to respond to a new patient care reimbursement policy. Reimbursement changed from a cost-based to a fixed-price system. In other words, health insurers would pay only a predetermined amount for a specific service, which could be considerably less than it cost the hospital to provide. Hospital management had to find ways to take care of patients cost-effectively so that the hospital's finances were not depleted by of the impact of the prepayment policy, which spread rapidly throughout the insurer network. In addition, the emergence of nonprofit hospitals was a threat to the traditional ones because they were more skilled in cutting costs and able to cope with the new rates.

By 1982 and 1983 planning had moved into the third stage: Strategic planning coupled with marketing became the new focus. Preparation for the new Medicare reimbursement policy along with the spread of the fixed-price system in general (e.g., health maintenance organizations) forced hospitals to develop their marketing research capabilities in order to collect the kind of information needed to make cost-effective business decisions. In 1983 the Tax Equity and Fiscal Responsibility Act (TEFRA) implemented the new limited-rate reimbursement by Medicare, called the prospective payment system (PPS). In effect, this Act mandated hospital reimbursement for Medicare patients in accordance with their diagnostic-related group (DRG) and the federally designated payment for that DRG, rather than the hospital's actual cost for providing the care.

The DRGs have had an enormous impact on planning because of the large numbers of Medicare recipients who receive hospital care. Hospitals require good information on the needs of the elderly population and how to plan for those services under the TEFRA restrictions. Cataract operations (to remove abnormal tissue that covers the lens of the eye), common among older patients, must be done as outpatient procedures because of the DRG rates. Changes in the provision of cataract procedures had to be made based on information that could guide the planning of cost-effective and quality care. If, for example, these procedures are performed on older persons living alone in the community, certain kinds of aftercare should be planned to assist those who might have difficulty caring for themselves during the recovery period.

Because of the new challenges, administrators of most major hospitals created high-level planning positions. By 1983 the positions of director or vice president of planning or planning and marketing had been established in many hospitals. Often the two functions are combined under a senior vice president for planning and marketing.

The *planning* function usually connotes long-term considerations: how the hospital should respond to changes in its environment through the next five or ten years. In contrast, *marketing* focuses on research and planning for short-term decisions. Planning identifies the broad scope of activities to be explored in response to trends in society, whereas marketing deals with specific programs, supplying research and evaluation. Both activities interact continually to strengthen the strategic planning process.

Professional Preparation

Hospital planners come from a variety of educational backgrounds. According to a recent survey, planners are likely to have master's degrees, mostly in fields other than business administration: 58 percent of responders indicated that they had "other" kinds of master's degrees.[1] Some have graduate credentials in public health, since most public health schools offer planning as part of their health management curricula. Other hospital planners have backgrounds in the social sciences. Graduate programs in urban or city planning with specialty health tracks are a source of academic preparation for many hospital planners.

The survey findings indicate that the responders in planning jobs have longer tenure in their positions than do those hired strictly for marketing positions. Eighteen percent of planners have been in health or hospital planning jobs for five years or more, compared to only 13 percent in marketing. Most of those currently in planning positions began their careers in planning. In contrast, marketing personnel came from a variety of planning, marketing, and public relations jobs. Of responders currently working in planning, 60 percent started in a designated planning position and another 20 percent indicated that planning constituted part of their responsibilities in their starting jobs.[1]

Talks with persons working in the field suggest that many hospital planners worked in other kinds of health organizations earlier in their careers. Some worked in federal, state, and local planning organizations, including those health systems agencies created by the 1974 planning legislation. Others worked for municipal health departments and professional associations performing a variety of planning functions such as collecting and analyzing data and designing community programs. Because some kind of planning activity occurs in most organizations, persons interested in careers in hospital planning can gain experience in a variety of health agencies and facilities.

In addition to acquiring the educational credentials and relevant work experience, persons interested in becoming hospital planners should learn as much as they can about health care delivery. For instance, applicants are more competitive if they know about the various programs and departments in hospitals and how they influence patient care. Demonstrating knowledge of the costs of care and reimbursement policies will impress administrators seeking competent personnel.

Planners need to be good at making projections on the basis of the information available to them. Educational programs and on-the-job training nurture this capability; but persons with a flair for putting together the right data on which to base their decisions are a step ahead as hospital planners. Often, judgments must be made quickly, and persons with a special knack for decisiveness can meet the challenge more easily and reap greater satisfaction from their work.

Good interpersonal skills are important, especially for persons directly involved in implementing change resulting from the planning process. Hospital planners need to know how to gain support for decisions that have hospitalwide effects on employees' activities and work styles.

Functions

Preparation for Planning.   Planning to achieve the hospital's long- and short-term goals is no longer based on the wishful thinking of hospital administrators or influential clinical staff and board members. It is a well-defined process that includes brainstorming among key personnel followed by designated activities performed by chief executive officers, committees, administrators, and staff.

In hospitals where no formal program has been established, planning is performed by individual department administrators working closely with financial management. Planning a new facility or modernizing or expanding existing space might be done by a consulting firm that specializes in health facility planning. Consultants in these instances work closely with the hospital administrator.

Although formal planning structures vary, the basic process used and functions performed are well defined. The planning committee is responsible for learning about the hospital system and its external environment. Committee members need to be well versed on community populations and trends that affect health care. The committee considers short- and long-term action alternatives and how each affects patient care and staff morale and productivity. It also explores procedures for ongoing evaluation of services and programs. Planning committees usually include the director of planning, the chairperson and members of the board of directors, medical staff, administrators, and frequently representatives of the community.

The Planning Process. The first major function of planning is to determine the role of the hospital, sometimes referred to as the *mission*. The planning committee, administrators, and key personnel need to know the characteristics of the population they serve, their health needs, and whether these are being filled satisfactorily. How does the hospital interact with other facilities, and is there an excess of certain services and programs in the area? How will the future affect the educational and clinical programs? Is the hospital prepared to make needed changes, and how will they affect the hospital's mission? Good answers to these kinds of questions will lead to determining a realistic mission, after which a meaningful planning program can be developed.

Planners can proceed by establishing short- and long-range objectives and services consistent with the mission. Objectives can be defined as specific aims or goals to be met in a given time period. If, for example, the mission includes meeting the health care needs of the community adjacent to the hospital, planners need to decide on the services and programs needed and some kind of schedule for their implementation. Depending on the financial resources available, a short-term objective might be to increase services for the elderly in the community. Care might be enhanced if part of an existing outpatient area were remodeled to be used exclusively for the primary care of geriatric patients. Such a project could be accomplished in a year. A longer-range objective might be to care for the homebound elderly in the neighborhood. A project to develop a home health care program over a two-year period run out of the geriatric center might be an appropriate service to meet this objective.

Realistic objectives need to be established hospitalwide, and departments must coordinate their plans to make possible their achievement. If, for example, the development of a geriatric center is planned, other hospital departments must coordinate their efforts and contribute to this objective. Nursing must designate staff and provide special training. The admissions department must modify its process to accommodate the needs of a new unit. Purchasing must order special equipment and furnishings. Planning effectively for the hospital means coordinating departmental efforts that complement the institutionwide mission and contribute to achieving the objectives that support it.

Some hospitals have developed a structured process for departmental interaction in planning and implementing projects. The process designates what should be done by department directors and top management on a monthly basis. For example, during the first month of planning a new project department directors meet with key planning personnel to review the mission, objectives, and project. In the next month department heads develop written objectives for their departments consistent with those discussed with the planning team. The month-by-month process continues until the final details, including budgetary considerations, are all in place and the project is ready to be implemented.

Because strategic planning is key in most hospitals today, the process is complicated by the need to explore alternatives constantly given possible changes in the resources available. Strategic planning is defined as "the process of implementing and making decisions concerning the use of resources to achieve an organization's goals and to fulfill its mission. [It]...is concerned with the alternative uses of resources rather than the immediate control of how targeted resources are spent.... Above all, it is concerned with how decisions made today will impact on the future of the organization."[2]

Identifying resources for the development of a program for the elderly, for instance, must be approached with the understanding that resources available for the project may change, and planning must consider several alternatives. Perhaps the remodeling of the geriatric unit will need to be postponed or changes be made in remodeling, kinds of equipment, and furnishings to cut project costs. Alternative plans must be developed simultaneously to permit initiation of the project even though the ideal version may not be possible.

Data Collection and Analysis. One of the most important functions of a hospital planner is the collection and analysis of data. The dictionary defines data as "facts, information, statistics, or the like, either historical or derived by calculation or experimentation." Data can be distinguished from *information* in that the latter is more likely to signify "knowledge communication or perceived concerning a particular fact or circumstance." The term data, then, refers to facts around which information is developed.

Much of the planners' time is devoted to gathering data and working with it to develop an information base (usually a combination of computerized and manual systems is used). The information is needed to help define the mission and objectives and to proceed with the planning of services and programs.

Planning staff collect many kinds of data in the hospital. They need facts about the services and programs offered and how well they are utilized. They need data on the patients who use the services as well as potential users. Planners keep aware of the daily census and changes in occupancy rates. They must know about the hospital employees, what they do, their educational backgrounds, and how they interact with each other professionally. Planners need to know the details of the organizational structure, staffing patterns in the various departments, and union regulations and their effect on programs. They must have access to medical reports: laboratory test results, surgical procedures performed, and many other kinds of data generated during diagnosis and treatment.

Planners strive for a comprehensive data system so that they can develop the kinds of information they need. If they want to modify the operations of an outpatient facility, for instance, they need specific data on staffing patterns, what is currently done in the unit, utilization, and other facts that make possible an effective plan for change. Planning staff must know what kinds of data to collect, where to find them, how to put them into a usable format.

Forecasting or Estimating Need. Comprehensive data collection and analysis enables planners to make projections and estimate the need for and utilization of future facilities, services, equipment, and manpower. First, planners must determine how far into the future they must project. The duration of short- and long-range planning varies among institutions: For some the short range is six months; for others it may be as long as two years. Planners must decide also how much data from the past is needed to make estimates for planning. The information required, its accessibility, and the cost of obtaining it determine how planners proceed when they make projections.

Implementation. Introducing change can be the most satisfying, and the most frustrating, experience of the hospital planner. Effective administrators keep clinical faculty and senior personnel informed of proposed changes throughout the planning process. They always solicit input from senior staff to make them feel close to the decision-making process and willing to back new projects with enthusiasm. In this way, good morale is promoted among employees, and new projects do not suffer because of the ambivalence that often discourages productivity.

Planners must be prepared to implement change carefully, even when faculty and senior staff have been included in the planning process. Timing is important, and planners must be sensitive to the readiness of clinicians and staff if they want to achieve their goals.

Evaluation. Sound planning efforts always include a system for ongoing evaluation. Hospital planners should add to their data base continually to help them appraise objectively their course of action and strategies. They must evaluate questionnaires from staff and patients and determine what changes need to be made. Past decisions must be questioned regularly. Are existing services adequate to meet needs: are they underutilized or used more frequently during some periods than others? Should certain underutilized services be eliminated? Are there ways to attract patients that would not have been effective during earlier stages of planning? These and many other questions need to be asked and answered.

Salary

Planning administrators are among the most highly paid professionals in the hospital. Positions held by responders to a recent survey who are older and of longer tenure are usually chief executive officers, vice presidents, or vice presidents for planning, and they tend to be the best paid. Vice presidents for planning average $50,500. Because of the way salaries were estimated in the study,* the average is actually probably higher. Younger responders (around 34) with less professional tenure are planning assistants and associates, with average salaries of $35,650.[1] Most entry-level personnel with one or two years of experience in a health organization and a bachelor's degree can expect to receive $25,000 to $28,000.

Job Outlook

Because planning is a high priority for hospital administrators, openings will continue for entry-level positions as well as those that require more extensive experience. Opportunities for persons with limited experience will be more widely available in smaller hospitals. The exception would be large city hospitals that have been slower to develop their planning departments and may need to catch up with their competitors.

Chances for advancement in the field are good because of the sophistication and knowledgeability of planning staff in the perceptions of chief executive officers and other key staff. The knowledge needed to function effectively in hospital planning, particularly at this time when strategic planning is essential, makes this a challenging career for persons stimulated by working with ideas and the excitement of developing solutions to key problems in hospital management.

References

[1] American Hospital Association, Society for Hospital Planning and Marketing, Summary, 1985 Membership Survey.

[2] Kropf, Roger, Ph.D., and Greenberg, James A., Ph.D. *Strategic Analysis for Hospital Management.* Aspen Systems Corporation, Rockville, Maryland, 1984.

Goldberg, Alan J., and DeNoble, Robert A. (eds). *Hospital Department Profiles.* American Hospital Publishing, Inc., 1986.

---

* Annual income averagea should be used for comparative purposes only, since responders gave a salary "range" and incomes over $60,000 were not recorded as such.

Chapter VI

Public Relations

Public relations is concerned with establishing and maintaining positive attitudes. It builds understanding between organizations and their communities. All organizations want to present an image that is attractive to their customers or clients. They also want to promote pride among their employees, improve morale, and enhance productivity. Public relations specialists use their skills and knowledge to achieve these goals.

In our complex society it is difficult for people to know about many of the influences on the policies and operations of most organizations. Understanding of the increasing numbers and kinds of issues that affect health care delivery and the operation of facilities that provide care is especially difficult to communicate to the public. Recent changes in how health care is provided, costs, and insurance reimbursement practices are bewildering to patients and make getting care a trying and confusing experience for many people. Hospitals are modifying the kinds of services they offer to adapt to these changes. Teaching the community about the issues that affect health care and the rationale behind the changes in services is a formidable challenge. Public relations specialists work to promote understanding in an effort to maintain the hospital's favorable image: one that projects caring and competence. They need to work more diligently than ever before in this era of rapid change.

Background

Unlike the other hospital careers discussed in this book, public relations work has been visible in many hospitals since the 1960s.

Some of the hospital administrators interviewed said that many of the functions associated with the field were performed regularly before that time by various administrators who were officially assigned to other jobs. One hospital director noted that as early as 1955 the director of nursing and some of her administrative staff frequently provided tours of the hospital and informational presentations about new services to patients and prominent visitors from the community. These are functions assumed routinely by public relations personnel at the present time.

Most facilities had no public relations specialists during the 1950s. By the early 1960s part-time employees were working in many hospitals, writing newspaper articles and providing information to the community. The area of responsibility encompassed a wide scope of activities often vague and difficult to define. It was not until the early 1970s that public relations departments were established formally as units within most hospitals, having discrete functions, policies, and procedures. Now, in larger hospitals (over 400 beds), almost half (47 percent) are separate departments, without functions associated with any other units.[1]

Public relations is at the basis of the interaction between personnel and the many people who walk through the hospital doors. Besides patients, their families, and visitors, these include pharmaceutical sales personnel, local politicians, community religious leaders, and news media representatives. The responsibility of public relations also includes promoting rapport among employees and helping to build morale. Effective interaction among workers in an organization enhances its image significantly.

Public relations specialists help personnel interact effectively with the community and with each other. They teach and encourage polite and helpful behavior and recommend appropriate dress to workers in jobs that have direct contact with the public. During the last decade the hospital's accountability to the public has escalated dramatically. The focus of activity of hospital departments has shifted from the earlier passive, poorly defined role to one that assumes an active position in communication with the media and in the development of policy for institutionwide priorities. The number of personnel working full time has increased as these activities have become more important to hospital administrators, reacting to pressures that go with being in the public eye. When events occur that might detract from a favorable image, public relations specialists work to minimize damage and restore the public confidence as quickly as possible.

The impact of public relations in the hospital touches upon all the factors that influence public opinion. Because of the increased competition among hospitals, public relations personnel have had to compete for the limelight in the community. Although program staff still perform a variety of functions, those activities that directly relate to establishing and maintaining the hospital's status assume priority. Public relations directors spend most of their time and effort defining hospitalwide interaction with the media, serving as cautious spokespersons, and promoting hospital achievements to a critical and perceptive audience.

Professional Preparation

Hospital personnel working in the field reflect considerable variety in educational backgrounds. Those who have been active for twenty years or more probably have no formal education in public relations. Typically, public relations directors have undergraduate degrees in journalism, English, the humanities, or social sciences. During the last decade colleges and universities have begun to offer coursework in public relations and communications; degree programs are available in increasing numbers of institutions. Sometimes they represent educational tracks within programs in departments of journalism or English.

Persons interested in obtaining a bachelor's degree in public relations can expect to receive a very practical orientation in most of the educational programs. Students learn how to write articles for a variety of publications and how to prepare and deliver public presentations. They study the publishing, news, and printing industries. They learn how to plan promotions, design and print pamphlets and brochures, and estimate advertising and managing costs.

Students are required to complete a supervised internship as part of most programs. Internships can be served in various kinds of organizations: some that specialize in public relations for private businesses and political campaigns; others that promote their own services and products.

Frequently, public relations personnel in hospitals pursue graduate degrees in business administration, marketing, journalism, or communications. A variety of such programs are available nationwide. The content of programs varies widely even when they have the same names; therefore, it is advisable to check admission requirements and course offerings as you investigate options. Most include courses specific to public relations, but some focus on developing administrative and research skills.

Public relations personnel in hospitals usually have substantial experience in other kinds of organizations, such as newspapers or public relations firms. Most directors have between five and ten years in the field before applying for a position. Recent information indicates that the average age of department directors is thirty-eight.[1] Experience in a health organization and especially in another health care facility is a valuable credential. Beginners are wise to gain such experience, if necessary as a student intern or as a volunteer.

Employers also look for special aptitudes and skills. They emphasize the importance of relating well to all kinds of people and the ability to work with them one to one or in a group situation. Physical stamina is also important because of the long hours required. The person who is comfortable with flexible hours is better able to accommodate to the irregular schedules associated with most work situations.

Ability to respond articulately and spontaneously is a challenge confronted frequently by hospital public relations specialists. Often they must serve as spokesperson for their organization, discussing complex issues without notice or preparation. Excellent communication skills are a must. If you are interested in a career in public relations, work to achieve good language skills for written and oral presentations.

Functions

Because of the broad interpretation of the public relations role in the hospital, functions of personnel continue to be extremely diverse in spite of the recent focus on image development.

A primary function of the director, one of increasing signifi-
cance because of the new priorities, is to organize hospitalwide
efforts and play a leadership role in developing and interpreting
policy. The director should serve as a central source of information
and guidance for hospital administration and staff who interact
with the public. He or she should have special expertise in working
with the news media and should be called upon to mitigate or
prevent crises that might affect the hospital's image.

In a leadership position, the director must be able to work with
top administration and the board in developing policy consistent
with institution by-laws and ethical considerations. Policy must be
carefully articulated and upheld, so that all hospital spokespersons
can promote a consistent image. This presents a special challenge
because administrative and physician staff interact directly with
the media and outside organizations and often neglect to discuss
their activities with public relations personnel. Many hospital administrators insist that all interaction between the hospital and the
media be monitored by the director of public relations to ensure
that policy is followed.

Public relations staff plan, design, and write promotional materials such as news releases, annual reports, patient and visitor hand-
materials or public presentations. Department staff may conduct
public and employee opinion surveys. Marketing research surveys
provide useful information for the public relations team.

Public relations staff plan, design, and write promotional materials such as news releases, annual reports, patient and visitor handbooks, in-house newletters, and pamphlets and brochures that
promote special events, services, or achievements. Marketing staff
may work with public relations personnel and assume some of the
responsibility for preparing publications directly related to the
marketing role. But public relations specialists assume the major
task of disseminating information to employees and to the community about achievements of and awards to hospital staff, special
research contributions, and new services and programs of interest
to the public.

Working with news media representatives, they present information programs for the community. These are often radio or
television shows, presented periodically or regularly. They plan
and hold press conferences and open houses, involving medical

staff and hospital administrators whenever appropriate. They organize and prepare displays in the hospital, at neighborhood events, or at various organizations. They often contribute to the preparation of exhibits at meetings of professional associations or for industries, promoting the latest advances in medical technology and research.

Public relations staff also organize and direct volunteer participation in special projects such as speakers' bureaus. They provide training for the volunteers to ensure that they are knowledgeable about the hospital's services and programs. The director of public relations has the responsibility for determining the readiness of volunteers to participate in public presentations. It is important that any person representing the hospital be knowledgeable about the services and programs so that they can respond to questions. They must also be familiar enough with policy to know which issues should be addressed only by designated hospital personnel.

Visitors' tours are frequently conducted by public relations personnel. They serve as goodwill ambassadors for patients and visitors as well as dignitaries who visit the hospital. Sometimes, visiting celebrities are hosted by city or state government, and hospital public relations staff interact with their personnel in presenting promotional events to coincide with the visits.

Hospital public relations staff also address civic, business, and service organizations and represent the hospital at community events. For example, the director might be asked to attend a conference on health education at the city's public health department and to give a presentation on the hospital's activities. A member of the health education staff may or may not be able to participate; sometimes public relations staff must serve without the assistance of others.

In the preparation of written material and publications, public relations personnel need photographs, historical documents, and various records and statistical data. They need to collect these materials and file them systematically so that they are easily accessible. When space is available, the department usually maintains a large library of documents and photographs for use by its own staff as well as others in the hospital.

Directors of public relations usually have many administrative responsibilities in addition to the functions described in the introduction of this book where general management tasks are addressed. Special functions of the public relations director include planning sessions with administration, the board of directors, and the physician staff. In these meetings policies and procedures are developed related to public accountability issues that arise. A newspaper article criticizing the actions of emergency room personnel in a disaster would alert administration to the need for a meeting of hospital administration, emergency room personnel, and the public relations director to prepare a statement justifying the actions taken.

In small hospitals the public relations department often has responsibility for a variety of other functions such as planning, marketing, or hospitalwide volunteer services. Recent information indicates that in about 31 percent of hospitals surveyed the planning, marketing, and public relations functions were housed in one department.[1] During the last decade, as demands on the public relations role have increased, the tendency to incorporate a variety of responsibilities within the department has decreased. Diversity, however, will always be characteristic of the public relations specialist's activity. The mix of functions provides interesting work for persons who can adapt to changing priorities among these many challenges.

Salary

Public relations directors at medium-sized to large hospitals earn between $32,000 and $40,000. Recent survey information reveals that the average salary is $37,250 for directors in the position for an average of five years.[1] Variations in salaries are influenced by educational credentials, amount and kind of experience, salary at the previous job, and general salary levels of the hospital. Smaller institutions, particularly in rural areas, tend to pay lower salaries and often hire part-time personnel, decreasing incomes further and often eliminating many of the fringe benefits enjoyed by full-time workers.

Entry-level salaries range between $22,000 and $28,000, assuming experience in the field. Most people work for at least a few years in public relations firms or for newspapers or advertising agencies, where they start at lower salaries and receive raises as they acquire on-the-job experience.

Job Outlook

Most sources indicate that prospects for employment in hospital public relations are especially favorable during the next decade. Because so many hospitals have been understaffed or without specific personnel in the past, these facilities will create new positions to more closely parallel staffing in other hospitals. In addition, the escalating competition between hospitals is expected to highlight the need for public relations experts.

Hospital public relations specialists can expect higher status and salaries in the future because of the emerging importance of maintaining image. Their increasing involvement with the highest levels of administration should allow for their input into most of the critical decisions in health care delivery and provide challenging and rewarding career opportunities.

References

[1] American Hospital Association, Society for Hospital Planning and Marketing, Summary: 1985 Membership Survey, 1986.

Chapter **VII**

Quality Assurance

At a time when cost containment is crucial to the survival of the hospital, senior administrators must be careful to avoid compromising the quality of patient care in their effort to maintain financial stability. They are as responsible for guiding quality assessment as they are for overseeing financial management. The chief executive officer, working with other senior administrators, must lead the development of a sound quality surveillance system. He or she needs to ensure that clinical and support services are provided in a professional manner, so that all aspects of the patient experience reflect the hospital's commitment to high standards.

Care can be divided into two main categories for purposes of assessing its quality. *Technical* care refers to the actual therapeutic and diagnostic treatment of patients. The *art-of-care* includes the many other aspects of the patient experience, primarily those that relate to the hospital environment and the attitude of the doctors and other members of the staff.[1]

To optimize technical care the physician seeks to improve his or her clinical skills, trying to identify medical problems more efficiently given the symptoms described by the patient or to interpret a diagnostic procedure more accurately, depending on his or her specialty. The physician who wants to improve the art-of-care works to effect good communication with patients and is attentive to their needs as persons.

It is important that technical care be monitored stringently and that medical problems be corrected as soon as identified. But the art-of-care also merits scrutiny because it is so closely linked to the

technical aspects and because it makes such an important contri
bution to the patient care experience.

The relationship between art-of-care and technical care is evident in the link between the sanitation precautions and the rate
of infection in a facility. But the total effort put forth by housekeeping staff and others in keeping the hospital clean also has an
impact on the patient's comfort and sense of well-being. Maintaining cleanliness, then, contributes indirectly to better technical
care and also improves the ambience of the hospital environment.

Staff from many departments in the hospital make contributions
to both kinds of care. Food service personnel, including dietitians, try to provide nutritious meals tailored to the dietary needs
of patients with different health problems. They also want to be
able to give patients palatable food to help counterbalance the
unpleasant aspects of the hospital stay. Physical therapists help
patients rehabilitate parts of the body and also counsel them on
how to improve their quality of life given the restrictions imposed
by their disabilities. Medical records personnel try to keep the patient's records accurate and current so that the data are available
for further diagnosis and treatment. They also make it possible
for patients to have copies of their test results and visit summaries
so that they can know more about their medical problems and
feel better able to contribute to decision-making regarding their
future care. The art-of-care standard is improved when consumers
can be made to feel that they have more control over their health
care.

Poor art-of-care has a significant impact on patients' perceptions
of their experience. Patients who wait for many hours in emergency rooms before they receive treatment, without an explanation
for the delay, feel that they have been deprived even when they
receive good technical care. Patients left unattended and improp-
erly clothed while they wait for X rays complain even when they
receive quality technical care from radiologists and their staff.
Poor communication between doctors and patients leaves lasting
impressions and is often cited as the real motivation for many
lawsuits that are not justified on the basis of poor quality technical
care.

In the current competitive environment, the patient's percep-

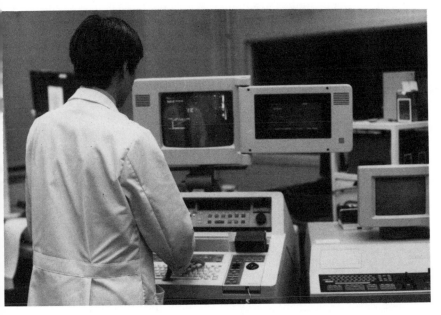

COURTESY DR. B. SIGEL
Good data storage systems are needed to maintain a stringently quality assurance program.

tion of the care received is particularly important. Monitoring the art-of-care is of increased interest among hospital administrators, regulatory agencies, and others in the field who are aware of its impact on the patient's experience.

Background

Quality audits and activities directed toward improving standards of care have been performed in hospitals for many years. Quality assessment studies have evaluated many aspects of technical care. Physicians used to work with other hospital staff, often untrained in evaluation methods and medical procedures, to complete reports responding to complaints by patients and their families or to meet requirements of regulatory agencies. The content of the assessment studies was limited as was the regularity of evaluation of care. Staff had little training in or dedication to quality assessment, and so the degree of activity depended solely on the enthusiasm of the individual physician or the chief of staff, whose responsibility it was to monitor the quality of care in the hospital.

During the last decade major changes have been made in quality assurance programs. The content of evaluation studies has been broadened markedly, to include not only a comprehensive assessment of the technical care but also of a much expanded list of art-of-care concerns.

Marked increases in the number of persons employed to assume quality assurance activities and changes in their training are other important differences that have evolved in recent years. Most hospitals have at least one employee whose major responsibility it is to coordinate quality assessment. Often this person is also responsibe for utilization review, the process of reviewing and recording changes in hospital occupancy rates and the use of services and programs. Many hospitals have sizable staffs that perform assessment activities. The director or coordinator of the quality assurance department works closely with the chief of staff, who oversees clinical care in the hospital.

Department personnel usually have some training in health care, and many are nurses with special preparation in evaluation methods. They must also know how to collect information and develop the hospital's quality assurance policies and procedures to conform to regulatory agency guidelines.

Quality assessment is a much more structured activity now than it was ten years ago. Several state health departments, professional standards review organizations, and the federal Health Care Financing Administration assess the quality of care rigorously. Third-party payers, a common term for health insurers, review quality and have begun to deny payment to hospitals that do not perform recommended procedures or provide good care.

Care is evaluated in many different ways within the structure. Methods vary in respect to the time period reviewed and whether they are those associated with prospective or retrospective study. They involve the use of various sources of data including patient records, questionnaire evaluation, interviews, and observations.

Different criteria on which to base evaluations are also used. Sometimes it is appropriate to assess patient care on the basis of the process used (for instance, the chain of procedures performed in response to certain symptoms). In other situations it is better to look at the outcome of treatment as the indicator of success or failure.

The auditing process is managed in one of three ways. Some hospitals use central audit committees with representation from the various clinical departments, medical records departments, nursing staff, and governing boards. Committee members perform much of the effort as a team.

Other hospitals have a central committee that distributes its function among committees within the individual departments, and these report to and work with the central group.

Another popular method of performing the auditing task is using an administrator to coordinate and oversee the activities of the various department that contribute to the monitoring process. For instance, an assistant chief of staff may work closely with a person who is in charge of coordinating the activities of the various departments. This person and the assistant chief of staff may work together to develop policy and procedures and report their progress to the chief of staff who oversees the total clinical performance.

Hospital staff work to ensure quality by using a three-step process. First, they focus on identifying the problem after they have analyzed the data that have been collected. This means that they review what happens in the hospital, identify trends, and single out recurring problems. The Joint Commission on the Accreditation of Hospitals (JCAH) and the Professional Standards Review Organization (PSRO) emphasize the importance of highlighting major problems through an effective auditing process.

The next step is to develop a plan for correcting problems and improving performance. The details of the plan depend, of course, on the findings of the audit process.

The final step is implementation. A structured process must be implemented within a designated time frame to ensure compliance with planned change and evaluation of its progress. This step is often difficult to carry out for obvious reasons pertaining to the introduction of change in any organization. In the hospital a power struggle usually is ongoing between influential clinical faculty, top administrators, and the governing board. Change favored by one or more of these groups may be challenged by another. Such conflict often postpones or prevents action and thwarts the implementation of change.

Implementation of change is accomplished most easily when doctors perceive that recommended changes are needed. The assessment process should lead to change in clinical practice, whether it relates to the technical or the art-of-care aspects. Because control of the implementation of change is not possible, most hospitals have a quality assessment as opposed to a quality assurance process. As internal and external pressures increase for improved standards of care, implementation of change gains more support from the power groups and quality assurance becomes a reality.

Professional Preparation

Quality assurance personnel come from many educational and experiential backgrounds, according to information from persons working in the field. Interviews with directors and coordinators of quality assurance indicate that they had had substantial experience in many of the tasks associated with quality assurance before they assumed administrative positions. Some were nurses working with central or departmental audit committees. Others had worked on evaluation studies of various procedures and services performed in the hospital.

Sometimes quality assurance administrators are also in charge of the risk management and utilization review effort. (Risk management is discussed in Chapter VIII.) These persons as well as administrators who perform only quality assurance functions are usually familiar with both roles. Even when they do not assume direct responsibility for these activities, they must be knowledgeable enough to work closely with those who do perform them. The quality assurance effort is tied to the total patient experience. If a patient slips and falls in a hallway, risk management personnel may be most active in placating the patient and investigating the mishap. However, quality assurance personnel inevitably become involved because of the implications of need for higher standards. If audit information indicates persistent safety problems related to the fall, quality assurance personnel interact with risk management staff to pursue solutions.

Nurses or persons with education in medical records management are among those likely to be working in quality assurance departments. Many community colleges and colleges of auxiliary medical sciences provide programs in medical record management. Because many nurses have substantial exposure to patient care management and the problems that arise in maintaining quality, they are popular candidates for quality assurance positions. As members of audit committees they also learn about procedure and policy requirements imposed by regulatory agencies and health insurers.

No statistical information is available on educational backgrounds of these personnel. Department administrators indicate, however, that more of their peers seek master's degrees in health-related fields.

Functions

The functions performed by quality assurance personnel depend to some degree on whether the hospital has a decentralized or centralized approach to quality control. As discussed earlier, many smaller hospitals have coordinators who serve as liaison between departments and the office of the chief of staff. Most larger hospitals have quality assurance departments where activities are more centralized and quality assurance staff perform most of the functions.

When the quality assurance function is decentralized, the person who serves in the coordinating role works with staff from the other departments to initiate the quality control process, guiding its development to conform with policies established by regulatory agencies and insurers. He or she may help them develop departmental programs by suggesting what should be audited, what methods and criteria could be used, and how to collect and organize the data. The coordinator might also make recommendations on establishing departmental quality control committees. Finally, coordinators pool the information that results from departmental activities and, working with the chief of staff, develop reports and other materials that document quality control activities and results.

In hospitals that use the centralized approach, the full-time director heads a quality assurance staff. Staff guide the collection of data within the departments or actually collect computer printouts and other materials needed to audit designated procedures and services. Staff choose the criteria to be used in assessing performance and analyze the data in respect to the criteria selected. When problems are identified, they bring them to the attention of the director and make recommendations for correction. They also request departments to provide additional data when needed. Staff also suggest new areas to be addressed: procedures and services that should be evaluated. They often initiate and perform studies of the procedures and services that they recommend. When staff are experienced in evaluation methology and data analysis, they can handle the audit of these areas with the approval of the departments. When staff do not actually perform the studies, they work closely with physicians and other health care professionals on developing studies relevant to the hospital's quality control goals.

All personnel involved in quality assessment try to find simple, timely, and inexpensive methods that do not disrupt patient care. If a study of the activities of busy medical practitioners is needed, methods that require minimal time investment are necessary. A chart of routine activities that can be checked off by doctors is a better mechanism, for example, than requiring them to keep a journal. Developing appropriate methods for studying quality is one of the most valuable contributions that can be made by quality assurance personnel.

Staff are also involved in implementing change. They help to educate the staffs of various departments regarding the policies of the external organizations that influence quality control. They work to promote hospitalwide support for modifications that have been designated to correct deficiencies. The role of staff in gaining the respect and trust of hospital employees cannot be overestimated.

The director of quality assurance, and sometimes members of his or her staff, work closely with the quality audit committee(s) described earlier. The committee works to improve standards by helping to coordinate hospitalwide activities, by informing and getting input from clinical departments, administration, and governing boards, and by recommending solutions for recurrent problems.

The committee's role does not include direct intervention. Instead it serves as a sounding board for discussing various quality control measures with assessment personnel, assists in decision-making, and gives support to the actions recommended. Because of the political power of many of its members, the committee has considerable influence on the decision-making process and is able to rally hospitalwide support for implementing change.

The director, with the assistance of staff, designs and adapts forms for displaying information that they collect and update these materials regularly. Charts or graphs that record information on medical records, utilization, and infection must be accurate and current and must be easily accessible to the audit committee and others who use them.

The director also acts to correct minor problems that are identified and reports on his actions at the executive committee of the medical staff. It is important that information from departments be coordinated, updated, and reviewed regularly so that small problems can be corrected quickly when possible. The quality assurance director oversees this process and can have a significant impact on eliminating everyday problems.

Quality assurance personnel, under the director's guidance, identify and employ new resources needed for developing solutions to problems. They develop questionnaires to be completed by patients, administrators, staff, and neighborhood groups. They provide suggestion boxes to encourage employees to share their ideas. Sometimes they assemble focus groups that study and make recommendations for solving special problems.

An example of a problem that might be studied by a focus group is physician and nurse resistance to observing isolation procedures designed to improve infection control. Assembling a group of people knowledgeable about a specific problem and having them work together to develop feasible solutions is often effective in addressing some of the difficulties that emerge in the quality control process.

Quality assurance directors perform the usual administrative functions and also assume some special management responsibilities. They provide inservice training for employees throughout the hospital, teaching them about quality assurance standards and how to develop studies relevant to their department's function.

Because they must interact with the many groups that contribute to the quality control process, they work to coordinate all the activities that are involved. They try to standardize data collection and reporting systems. They work with the audit committee(s) and with the chief of staff, keeping them informed on all ongoing activities.

Salary

A recent survey revealed that personnel working in the field make between $20,000 and $27,600 in small hospitals, $23,000 to $37,500 in medium-size facilities, and $26,900 to $46,100 in the larger hospitals[2]* As is true of many hospital jobs, the pay scale is influenced by the size of the facility. Although specific information is not available that links salary levels with facility sites, usually hospitals in large metropolitan areas pay more than do those in small towns.

Job Outbook

As external pressures increase, initiated by both the regulatory agencies and insurers, there will be a need for more persons skilled in quality assurance functions. More staff will be needed to collect and analyze the additional data that are required and probably more to develop the studies recommended. Both entry-level personnel and those with more extensive training will be in demand. Hospitals in which quality assurance is now a decentralized proc-

---

* Information on salary levels is available only for hospital personnel who perform both the risk management and quality assurance functions.

ess may decide to establish a special department and will need to staff it. Those that have existing departments may need more entry-level people to help collect additional data or persons skilled in evaluation methods to work on the new studies that will be developed.

References

[1] Rowland, Howard S. and Beatrice L. *Hospital Administration Handbook*, Aspen Systems Corporation, Rockville, 1984.
[2] American Hospital Association, ASHPA Management Compensation Study, Chicago, 1985.

Chapter VIII

Risk Management

The doctor-patient relationship, characteristically, has been one in which the patient assumed a submissive role. Becoming sick meant relinquishing everyday responsibilities and autonomy. Patients complied with the doctor's directions as closely as possible, always trusting his judgment and never challenging his authority. The patient believed that when something went wrong it must be attributable to phenomena beyond the control of the doctor: fate or limitations in the progress of science. Few if any malpractice suits were brought against physicians: Patients simply did not link the doctor's negligence or incompetence with unfavorable treatment outcomes.

As the consumer movement became more powerful and outspoken, particularly during the last decade, the accountability of the medical profession to the public has spiraled. The traditional doctor-patient relationship has been challenged. Patients are not willing to give up their autonomy: they want to be partners with the doctor in making decisions about their care. Their expectations are high: They believe that there is a cure for most ailments, and they hold the physician responsible when satisfactory outcomes are not achieved. When something goes wrong now, patients are less likely to fault the progress of science or technology. They are ready, sometimes even eager, to fault their doctor's decisions and performance. Most patients understand that there are certain risks involved in getting care, even when their doctors are competent and caring. But beyond certain minimal limits they hold physicians responsible for poor outcomes.

There is justification for some of the blame that has been leveled at the medical community. It is estimated that about one percent of all inpatients have cause to sue physicians who care for them and would probably win compensation if they did.[1] Since about forty million persons are hospitalized annually, the numbers affected are thus substantial. Some of them sue; others do not.

Besides the legitimate complaints that develop into litigation, large numbers of unfounded malpractice suits plague physicians and other providers of care. Poor rapport between the doctor and the patient can culminate in unfounded claims, even when an unimportant mishap occurs. A typical flagrant abuse of legal action is the *umbrella suit*, in which every health professional connected with a case is sued, from the plastic surgeon who actually performs cosmetic surgery to the resident and operating room nurse who assist during the procedure. Often, expectations regarding treatment outcome are so high that satisfaction of the patient is not a realistic goal. Patients may try to sue when they are disappointed. In this increasingly adversarial climate, lawsuits are pursued with little or no provocation.

Not only has the number of malpractice cases doubled during the last ten years, but the size of awards has increased almost ten times between 1975 and 1982. In a study conducted by the National Association of Insurance Commissioners, the average malpractice award in 1975 was $26,565; by 1982 it had leaped to $217,836.[1]

The increase in number of malpractice suits and amount of money awarded has had an enormous influence on the costs of care, the doctor-patient relationship, and the shortages in certain medical specialty areas. Its contribution to costs has sometimes crippled hospitals and practitioners. The increased cost of malpractice insurance by physicians and health facilities is reflected in the patient's bill. Physicians have been intimidated into performing unnecessary tests and other procedures to protect themselves with extra documentation in case a patient sues. The trust between doctor and patient has been eroded. Medical students shy away from fields in which lawsuits are frequent and insurance rates are high. Shortages of obstetricians and gynecologists persist in many parts of the country because of the high insurance rates and the exodus of physicians from the specialties because of them. Doctors elect other specialties or leave the practice of medicine altogether.

Clearly, the incentives are strong to bring the malpratice crisis under control. The role of risk management personnel in the hospital is dictated by this urgency. Risk managers work to reduce suits against the hospital and its health care providers. They negotiate with dissatisfied patients and their families to prevent litigation. They counsel physicians and other members of the staff who are involved in suits and instruct them regarding the prevention of future claims and litigation. They keep accurate records that document incidents, so that if claims are filed the necessary information is available. The role of the risk manager has become a key one in protecting the financial security and the image of the hospital.

Background

Because risk management professionals are relatively new in the hospital, little was known about their function until the last few years. In 1977 the American Hospital Association invited hospital risk managers to special meetings as part of its workshop program on institutional malpractice prevention, in an effort to find out more about their problems and needs. It was found that of the 51 risk managers who attended the meetings about half (28) had some training in hospital administration. Many had training in insurance (15); others, in business-related fields (5), nursing (4), personnel administration (3), and a few in law and medicine (2). They had dissimiliar backgrounds, and most had been employed by the hospital in other positions (35) before assuming risk management roles, for which some had little or no preparation.

Their authority and support were extremely limited among administration and medical staff. Most risk management personnel reported their findings about investigated injuries to the department head where the incident occurred (36), and they generally had limited access to top administrative staff or legal counsel for policy-making contributions. Most had no staff other than secretarial (23) and spent only part of their time in risk management activities (36). They usually had limited input into decision-making. Most of their function consisted of investigating injuries and reporting their findings. Some were involved in claims management (35), a substantial number were asked to evaluate their hospital's insurance program (31), and several purchased their hospital's insurance policy (20). Few maintained liaison with their hospital's insurer. They served on a wide variety of hospital committees but were not able to provide the input that they could have if they were involved in a more comprehensive risk management program.[2]

Risk managers at the AHA meetings expressed the need for more data from internal and external sources and the opportunity to have more input into decision-making, such as reviewing hospital contracts before signing. They wanted to be able to implement preventive procedures, including the education of staff, and they complained of lacking support from medical staff and administration to develop the comprehensive programs necessary for effective risk management.[2]

More recent information indicates that by the early 1980s risk management activity had achieved a much higher status. According to a study reported in 1984, responsibility for the role was most often assumed by senior officers or vice presidents (28 percent), chief executive officers (15 percent), or coordinators or directors of risk management programs (16 percent). (Some responders indicated that they continued to have only part-time employees without administrative titles performing these functions.) When risk management functions are performed within a special department under a coordinator or director, these administrators tend to report to the highest levels of management: to chief executive officers or to vice presidents (75 percent). Risk management personnel now have ongoing interaction with hospital insurers and in-house legal counsel. Directors work closely with legal counsel and the medical staff to maintain a comprehensive risk management program.[3]

Program activities have expanded significantly. Staff has been increased because, as noted, the functions of personnel are more numerous and because potential and actual suits are more prevalent. The average number of staff directly supervised by the director is 3.5. Larger departments that provide more record-keeping, data collection, and retrieval activities average about 14 staff members.[3]

Department administrators assume significant authority and responsibility in comparison to their earlier counterparts. Almost 43 percent of responders to the recent survey helped to select insurance brokers, and 46 percent helped to choose insurance carriers for their hospitals. Over 6 percent indicated that they had complete authority for making these decisions. Almost 49 percent had full responsibility for risk financing. Most took over the management of their departments (66 percent) and had full or shared responsibility for the group insurance plan (84 percent), risk identification and evaluation (95 percent), loss prevention (94 percent), patient complaints with potential risk of suits (96 percent), product liability claims on those filed because of faulty equipment or materials (89 percent), and the design and administration of other employee benefit packages (84 percent). The level and expanded scope of the authority of risk managers represents an important change in the role that has evolved during the last decade.[3]

Professional Preparation

According to the recent survey, risk management staff have substantial backgrounds in health care in contrast to those informally surveyed six years earlier. On the average, they have worked for fourteen years in health or closely related fields such as gerontology or social work. Responders to the survey had averaged more than four years in their present position as risk manager and eight years employed as health professional by the hospital where they are currently working.

Health care administration is most frequently reported (46 percent) as the responders' perception of their professional discipline, with health care (19 percent) and personnel management (7 percent) as the second and third choices. It appears that risk managers see themselves as definitely linked with the health management team, suggesting, as other information confirms, that their role has been expanded and has achieved higher status in the hospital. More than 6 percent of the responders indicated that their professional designation was as a fellow or member of the American College of Hospital Administrators, adding support to their closer affiliation with the health care management category.[3]

Although no information is available on the educational levels of risk managers in the 1970s, many responders said that they had replaced employees who had less formal education. More than 37 percent of responders have master's degrees, the highest level of education most frequently reported. About 32 percent have bachelor's and 8 percent associate degrees.

Although a broad spectrum of educational backgrounds is represented in the survey responses, degrees in health care administration are the most frequent academic credentials: More than 22 percent of the responders indicated that it had been their field of study. Many had degrees in business administration (19 percent) and nursing (13 percent). These are the three most numerous academic credentials among responders. Other areas of study include the social sciences, law, allied health, and accounting.

In addition to a solid orientation to health care management, through experience and formal education, persons interested in careers in hospital risk management should cultivate certain other abilities and skills. Because of the sensitive nature of much of their work, they need good interpersonal skills that can enable them to criticize in a constructive manner. They are often called upon to counsel medical staff and other hospital employees regarding their interaction with peers and the public. They must be able to identify and minimize problematical behavior without being offensive, communicating with a broad variety of people of diverse educational and social backgrounds. They must be articulate, able to interact on a one-to-one basis or to state difficult concepts simply to groups of employees during committee meetings or in educational sessions. They must be meticulous in investigation of incidents and recording of the relevant details. Risk management personnel are often among the first persons notified of accidents or other problems, so they must be sensitive and cautious regarding the sharing of information. They need to maintain confidentiality and at the same time report mishaps to key individuals who need to be aware of potential claims or suits.

Functions

Risk managers focus on developing and carrying out a comprehensive program that reduces the number and size of liability

Presentation of a fire prevention program by risk management personnel.

claims against the hospital. This effort involves considerable counseling and educational activity. Personnel frequently cooperate with other departments, such as safety management, in the presentation of programs for employees. Working with the safety officer, risk managers develop and present programs on accident prevention, proper disposal of waste products, and how to use back and leg muscles in such a way as to prevent back problems. Risk managers advise physicians and other personnel when litigation is brought against them. They often present workshops for physicians relevant to modifying their behavior so as to discourage future claims. Increasingly, physicians seek the advice of risk management personnel. Medical staff have begun to appreciate input from risk managers as valuable assistance for improving their practice.

Risk management personnel also counsel employees regarding their rights and the procedures for claiming workers' compensation. They work with patients and visitors who have complaints about their treatment or have accidents in the hospital, attempting to compensate victims justly, eliminating the need for legal intervention whenever possible.

The investigative function remains an important one. Risk managers cooperate in investigating losses of valuables reported by patients. They try to trace the pathway of items through the system: checking to see if missing eyeglasses and other items were picked up on a food tray or spotted in the soiled linen room. When items are not found they assist patients by providing funds to purchase replacements. Some hospitals have eliminated or put a limit on the replacement of valuables, insisting that patients are cautioned not to bring them to the hospital. The loss of items of value that patients need while they're hospitalized, such as hearing devices and glasses, continues to be a problem in implementing this policy.

Risk managers also investigate problems involving injuries of staff, patients, and visitors. They investigate the complaints by interviewing those who witness injuries and by reviewing all records relevant to a case. They document their findings thoroughly, so that a complete account of every incident is available when it is needed. They handle the processing of compensation for victims of accidents, attempting to minimize bad feelings and prevent future claims and lawsuits.

The following represents a typical incident report that could be sent to risk managers.

A 63-year-old woman with a 12-year history of high blood pressure but no documented heart disease was transferred from a suburban hospital to receive a cardiac catheterization procedure. She had been advised to seek treatment because of shortness of breath and frequent episodes of chest pain during the last few months. During the catheterization, medical staff had difficulty passing the balloon tubing through the patient's artery. Staff immediately followed the manufacturer's emergency instructions by injecting a small amount of air through the tubing. Air was seen free outside of the balloon, indicating a tear in the balloon. The patient began to have seizure activity. Emergency procedures were put into effect, the patient was stabilized and the catheterization was completed. Thereafter the patient had left-side paralysis and was transfered to a rehabilitation center.

In anticipation of a complaint or possible litigation, risk management personnel would initiate a series of activities aimed at explaining and documenting the course of action taken by the clinical staff. Typically they would include:

1. Notifying the patient representative staff, who would assist the patient and family by providing information and helping to alleviate anxiety.

2. Establishing a legal file on the case that contained a copy of the medical record and documentation of the actions taken by the clinical staff and risk management. The documentation would consist of a detailed report indicating that: medical records personnel had placed the medical record in the legal lock-up drawer (to maintain confidentiality), the manufacturer of the balloon had been contacted, the defective equipment had been secured for evidence if and when needed, and an evaluation and report on the defective equipment had been sent to the manufacturer.

3. Presenting a summary of what happened, clinically as well as risk management's follow-up, at the Incident Review Committee for review and recommendations for further action. (Members of this committee include key personnel such as the safety officer and the legal counsel.)

The investigation and documentation of injuries to employees and patients are carefully performed by risk managers so as to provide information to protect the hospital's interests in the event that excessive compensation is requested or legal action is pursued.

Risk managers also evaluate insurance plans, often assuming responsibility for selecting and managing group insurance plans and employee benefit claims. They work closely with insurers, keeping them up-to-date on all actual and potential litigation against the hospital. The constant exchange of information between risk managers and insurers is critical to the development and maintenance of good relations. Insurers who experience good communication gain trust in the administration and are more likely to believe that it acts prudently in the hospital's interests. Such trust can help minimize insurance rates while maximizing protection for the hospital.

Risk management personnel are involved in a variety of other functions to protect the institution and its employees. They design and administer employee benefit packages, including provisions for health care. They make recommendations to security personnel, safety administration, and other units to make the hospital a more secure environment. For instance, the risk manager may be aware of assaults on personnel that occur in a specific area inside the hospital or on the grounds and suggest that better lighting or more security personnel should be provided.

Risk management personnel spend considerable time at committee meetings sharing their information with persons who need to be knowledgeable about risks in the hospital environment. They are active participants on patient relations, safety, and other committees that develop policy and procedures.

Directors of risk management perform the administrative functions associated with staff supervision, budget management, and departmental planning discussed earlier in the book. They are spokespersons for their department at hospitalwide decision-making committees. Because of the nature of their input, they require special sensitivity to the need for confidentiality while they provide needed information to their peers.

Risk management personnel are also valuable sources of information for medical staff, top administration, and other employees. Increasingly, the value of a comprehensive risk management program is becoming apparent to those who formerly were reluctant to provide the support that risk managers need to function effectively.

Salary

Incomes of risk management personnel have risen substantially within the last six years, according to the recent AHA study. Although there are no published survey data on earnings in the 1970s, interviews with persons working in the field at that time suggest that most directors were paid around $25,000 and most staff earned between $18,000 and $22,000. More than 52 percent of risk management personnel responding to the recent survey earned more than $20,000, with 17 percent reporting salaries between $30,000 and $34,999. Almost 10 percent earned between $40,000 and $44,999, and another 4 percent between $45,000 and $49,999. Neither hospital size nor region of the country seemed to influence the income of the 52 percent that represented the largest group of responders.[3]

Although the results were not reported in such a way as to link salary levels with administrative titles, it is probable that the highest earnings are of vice presidents, presidents, or chief executive officers. Almost 8 percent of responders indicated that their salaries were between $50,000 and $69,999, consistent with the range of earnings reported by senior hospital administrators.[3]

For most risk management personnel, salary levels depend on experience and educational levels attained. Academic credentials appear to be increasingly important in this discipline, so that persons with advanced degrees have some edge in competing for available positions.

Job Outlook

Opportunities for employment in the field are excellent for persons with competitive credentials. Not only are the sizes of department staffs increasing, but it is probable that positions will be created in hospitals that currently do not have full-time risk managers. The AHA estimates that about 73 percent of all hospitals have a designated staff position with risk management responsibilities.[3]

Because of the growing pressure from litigation, risk management will continue to play a key role. More qualified administrators and staff will be needed to assume these responsibilities that have become so critical to effective hospital management.

References

[1] Cassidy, Robert. "The Law: Poor Remedy for Bad Medicine," *Chicago Reader,* Nov. 19, 1982, V. 12, #8, p.10.

[2] Korsak, Andrew. "Hospital Risk Managers Have Diverse Backgrounds," American Hospital Association, Department of Employee Relations and Training, October 8, 1977.

[3] American Society for Hospital Risk Management and the Department of Special Surveys, American Hospital Association, Hospital Data Centers, Summary Report "Survey of Risk Management Responsibilities and Salaries, 1983," April, 1984.

Chapter **IX**

Safety Engineering

The workplace can be an unsafe and unhealthful environment. Faulty equipment, careless work patterns, mental and physical stress, lack or misuse of protective garments, and contamination from toxic substances are among the most common threats to workers' health.

Since the late nineteenth century the numbers of on-the-job injuries and accidental deaths have escalated dramatically in the United States. By 1955 the death rate from industrial accidents had risen to 24 per 100,000 workers.[1] Factory workers, many of whom were women and children, operated unsafe machinery in poorly lighted and unventilated space, often for twelve and fifteen hours a day. Workers were crowded together in dilapidated offices and factories and frequently returned to substandard housing at the end of their long work day.

During this period some national and state laws were passed to improve safety and health standards. Many of these laws limited the number of hours a person could work. In 1886, New York passed a law regulating the employment of women and children in factories and requiring regular inspections of worksites. Before that time it was common to see seven- and eight-year-olds working twelve- to fourteen-hour days.[2] Other laws provided compensation for work-related injuries and disease. The Federal Employers' Liability Act was passed by Congress in 1908, making railroads and other interstate carriers liable for job injuries sustained by their employees. Before the passage of the Liability Act, only one out of eight injured men received any compensation and the amount actually paid was only about a third of what was awarded.

Ongoing inspection of the hospital's physical plant.

The year 1911 marked the beginning of major steps toward progress: Ten states passed workers' compensation laws, introducing a new era when employers increasingly became responsible for the medical and surgical care of their employees who were injured or became ill on the job.[1] Although early legislation represented a start toward coping with the deplorable conditions, needless accidents, deaths, and work-related illness continued to victimize thousands of industrial workers. Not until the late 1960s did the incidence of fatal industrial accidents decline significantly. By 1969 the rate had dropped to 18 per 100,000 persons, and it leveled off at 14 per 100,000 in the late 1970s.[2] Although deaths and injuries associated with the use of machinery have continued to decline during the last twenty years, illness attributable to conditions in the work environment is increasing, particularly the kinds of disease that are diagnosed only after many years of exposure to toxic substances. Emphysema and other lung problems are often caused or exacerbated by continuing exposure to toxic fumes and materials endemic to certain work environments.

Background

Although hospitals are not among the worksites that present severe occupational health risks to employees, certain safety and health hazards exist. Many employees work long hours standing or sitting in one position, contributing to the range of muscular and neurological problems evidenced in this population. Some workers endure particularly debilitating physical as well as emotional stress. The surgical nurse, for example, stands in the operating room for long periods of time while assisting in the care of patients with life-threatening illness. Physical stress comes from the standing, often in the same position, without breaks for food or relaxation. The added strain of having responsibility for the care of critically ill patients often contributes to the development of severe emotional problems.

Other workers are exposed routinely to infectious diseases brought into the hospital by patients, visitors, or other employees. Some workers have regular exposure to radiation and to patients who receive radiation treatments. Radiologists and X-ray technicians perform diagnostic and therapeutic procedures that require continuing contact with patients during their care. Many hospital jobs require strenuous activity: Employees must move quickly, work six or eight hours without breaks, and lift patients and heavy objects. Some work frequently with unfamiliar equipment, because the technology changes so rapidly that they have limited time to keep up with new diagnostic and therapeutic equipment.

Workers are often unaware of the hazards to which they are exposed routinely. Even when they perceive that some of their functions are threatening to their health, they are unwilling or do not know how to take precautions.

For many years infectious disease and radiation exposure were the acknowledged risks for hospital employees. During the last ten or fifteen years, however, awareness of many other occupational hazards has heightened. The Joint Commission on the Accreditation of Hospitals has developed safety standards with specific recommendations to help guide the development of programs tailored to the needs of individual facilities. Among the recommendations was establishment of safety committees and development of programs for employee training and education, fire warning systems, safe disposal of hazardous materials and wastes, and use of safety devices and practices. To accomplish these tasks, more hospitals have employed safety personnel in recent years.

Safety officers, sometimes titled safety directors or administrators, implement national and state agency standards and work to make hospitals more healthful places for employees, patients, and visitors. They investigate safety and health problems and bring them to the attention of the administration. Safety officers make recommendations on the proper lighting of hallways and patient rooms, disposal of waste matter, and control of noise in patient areas. They often work closely with administrators and architects during the development of plans for building modifications or additions. Safety officers might be asked to participate in aspects of the decision-making process when a new patient care wing is added, with reponsibilities ranging from inspecting plumbing installations to assisting in the selection of furniture and window and floor coverings. The scope of responsibilities is broad, but certain persistent problems have emerged as priority concerns of safety officers.

Safe handling and disposal of hazardous wastes is a major issue in most hospitals. The disposal system is monitored to insure its conformity to national and state environmental control policies. These regulate how hazardous material flows through the system so as to minimize exposure of employees and patients before it reaches the destination where it is incinerated or buried. Asbestos and radiation are two of the most harmful sources of contamination in the hospital. Safety officers make sure that employees recognize asbestos and report suspected samples. (Asbestos insulation is no longer used in new construction.) It is important that employees become knowledgeable about hazardous wastes and recognize safety risks.

Another current concern of safety personnel is smoking in the hospital, which is harmful to smokers as well as other employees who work with them. The increased risk of heart disease, emphysema, and other health problems has resulted in the prohibition of smoking or limitation of areas where people may smoke. Smoking is also a problem because of the increased risk of fire that it presents. Fire prevention and safe evacuation planning are ongoing activities in most safety programs.

Back problems and other conditions caused by physical and emotional stress are another focus of safety personnel. AIDS (acquired immune deficiency syndrome) is a new threat. Personnel who work directly with AIDS patients need to know how to minimize risk to themselves and others.

Additional to these national concerns for occupational safety, a variety of problems peculiar to individual communities become concerns of safety personnel. Local toxic substance dumps, water supply contaminants, and other problems are investigated routinely.

Professional Preparation

Specific preparation for safety personnel is not widely available at the college level. A few universities offer concentrations in the environmental sciences, but such programs afford limited opportunity for practice in the sampling and testing of toxic substances or other practical tasks. Several recent studies have cited the need for programs in industrial hygiene at the undergraduate level, where students could focus on the study of toxic substances in the workplace and serve internships in industry to gain firsthand familiarity with the functions performed by safety personnel.

Most safety officers currently working in hospitals have undergraduate degrees in engineering or the biological or physical sciences. They often work for a time in industry or governmental agencies to gain practical experience. Master's and doctoral programs in schools of public health offer specialized degrees in environmental and occupational health with extensive internship experiences for students. If you are interested in acquiring academic credentials (or advanced courses in nondegree programs), consult the catalogs of the various schools and colleges to determine what preparation you need and what programs fit your career goals.

A career in hospital safety requires a variety of skills in addition to those pertinent to scientific preparation. Knowledge of the special kinds of risks in the hospital environment and an understanding of the health care delivery system are important. Safety officers must be aware of the relation of their role to the care of patients and to the work of other hospital employees.

Frequently the safety officer or coordinator is the only hospital employee with the special expertise to recognize and deal with occupational health problems. He or she must be able to function independently and know whom to contact when outside expertise is needed. Management abilities are necessary, as much so for those officers who supervise a staff as for those who work alone and single-handedly deal with the many priorities of administration. Rapport with all kinds of people is a must, so the development of strong interpersonal skills is essential.

Functions

Safety personnel perform a great variety of functions and often must choose between priorities in crisis situations. They investigate the causes of accidents and make recommendations for system or facility changes to minimize recurrences. If patients or employees frequently fall in a particular area of the hospital, it is the responsibility of safety personnel to determine whether the lighting, the floor surface, or other factors are involved and to make recommendations to correct the condition that contributes to the problem.

Safety personnel work closely with risk managers and their staff in the investigation of accidents in the hospital. They discuss their findings relevant to specific accidents with risk management and patient relations personnel or hospital administration, so that these persons have the information they need to manage problems effectively. They constantly inspect the hospital environment for safety or health hazards so that these can be eliminated or minimized before injuries occur.

An important function of the safety officer is to monitor the waste disposal system for conformity to standards established by environmental agencies. They inspect plumbing installations and check that waste is packaged according to standards and sealed in protective containers if infectious. They monitor all parts of the system routinely to ensure the safe transport of hazardous materials through the hospital.

Sometimes safety officers have not had the necessary training to deal with the safe disposal of radioactive materials or radiation exposure. In these instances they work with specialists, either on their staff or employed in the radiology department, to protect patients, laboratory personnel, and other at-risk employees.

Safety personnel who specialize in handling radiation exposure problems are often called health physicists or radiological physicists. They study the hospital environment to develop inspection standards, radiation exposure limits, safe work methods, decontamination procedures, and tests for all areas of the hospital to insure that radiation never exceeds safety standards. They consult with scientists about new experiments to determine if hospital equipment and space design conform to the latest safety guidelines. They instruct personnel on precautions against radiation hazards, and they demonstrate proper equipment operation, decontamination techniques, and emergency procedures. Finally, radiation specialists prepare reports on the analysis of hazards and recommend improved methods of radiation control throughout the hospital.

An important aspect of the safety officer's role is to make all hospital employees aware of risks in their environment and teach them how to change their behavior to protect themselves. Of pressing concern is restricting the spread of AIDS. Safety officers run workshops for employees who have regular contact with AIDS patients. They instruct nurses about disposal of materials contaminated by patients' blood and advise maintenance and housekeeping staff regarding contact with solid wastes.

Back injuries are a persistent problem for hospital employees. Safety personnel teach on a one-to-one basis and conduct workshops on how to lift patients properly, how to do exercises that reduce physical and emotional stress, and how to maintain good posture when standing or sitting in one position for long periods of time.

Safety officers place special emphasis on educating employees about smoking in the hospital environment. Smoking is permitted only in designated areas. Rooms where people may smoke become fewer as more nonsmokers complain about the risks to their health from secondhand smoke. Safety officers make employees aware of actions to be taken in the event of fire and provide frequent workshops on fire prevention. The risk of fire in the hospital has been minimized significantly in recent years by the installation of detection and warning systems and the fire prevention education that safety personnel provide.

Safety officers are responsible for keeping informed about local safety and health problems. They keep abreast of hazards in the community and investigate their presence in and impact on the hospital environment. For example, if a local department of health reports that high levels of lead have been found in some part of the community's water supply, safety personnel in area hospitals test samples of water promptly to see if hospital supplies have been contaminated. If they have been, employees must be informed immediately of precautions they must take to protect patients, visitors, and themselves.

Safety officers function as manager of their programs and assume the administrative functions discussed earlier. Among other

Inspecting a machine for safe operation.

management functions, they often must train hospital employees other than their own staff about maintaining hospital safety standards. They instruct housekeeping personnel, for instance, about the identification and proper disposal of toxic or infectious materials. They teach employees how to investigate and keep accurate records of accidents. They are also responsible for collecting information necessary for hospital accreditation and for confirming compliance with environmental standards established by government agencies. This aspect of their management role is increasingly demanding as government regulation of occupational safety and health continues to require greater accountability.

Salaries

Entry-level safety personnel earn about $23,000 to $26,000, depending on their educational credentials and experience. Safety officers or directors usually make between $40,000 and $50,000, depending on their educational background and the length and quality of their on-the-job training. Persons who have had significant training in industry, where salaries are generally higher than in many government agencies, often are recruited by hospitals at higher salaries. Because most persons who are hired as safety officers come to the hospital with substantial experience in occupational health, they are in demand in a variety of work settings, and salaries reflect the need for their specialized expertise.

Job Outlook

Prospects for employment as safety personnel are extremely good as hospital administrators continue to recognize the necessity for these workers. Although the Joint Commission for the Accreditation of Hospitals has not mandated full-time safety personnel, it is expected that accreditation requirements will include safety employees in the near future. Currently, the Joint Commission does require that all hospitals and psychiatric facilities have safety committees and that safety officers be members.

Regulatory constraints imposed by federal, state, and local authorities indicate the increasing concern for the safety of patients and hospital employees. This concern is expected to generate the need for more and better-trained safety staff.

References

[1] Hanlon, John J. *Public Health Administration and Practice* (6th ed.). C.V. Mosby Co., Saint Louis, 1974.

[2] Ford, Amasa. *Urban Health in America.* Oxford University Press, New York, 1976.

Chapter **X**

Getting the New Jobs

A book about new careers in the hospital would not be not complete without information on how to get started on finding a job. *You need to find out what positions are available in your area and learn as much as possible about them.*

Unless you are willing to relocate, in which case you might want to consult recruitment firms in the city of your choice, you should explore all the resources available in the community where you live. These include:

- Local and neighborhood newspaper ads.
- Friends and professional associates and their network of acquaintances working in the health field.
- Personnel departments of hospitals.
- Journals for health professionals. (Many have special sections on jobs available in the field.)
- Job clearinghouse centers, frequently located at hospital association or professional organization offices.
- Career services at colleges and universities.
- Professional recruiters.

Talk to knowledgeable people about what you want to do, your qualifications, and what academic credentials or experience you need to be competitive in the field.

Friends or professional associates working in hospitals, human resource personnel, and career counselors who specialize in health can supplement the information contained in this book. You need to decide whether to return to college or university for a degree or to take special courses relevant to your interest. Perhaps it is advisable to study part time and work or volunteer in the field while you enhance your formal education? Talk to people in the field about their academic and experiential preparation, and ask them to assess its role in expanding opportunity in the field.

If you decide to continue your education, explore objectively the academic program options that are available.

If you decide not to relocate to earn a degree or take courses, explore all the resources in your community and talk to faculty and career advisers about your interests. Their perspective on their institution's curricula can help guide your selection process.

The decision to relocate so that you can enroll in a particular college or graduate program should be made only after a careful review of the options. Contact professional organizations in your field of interest for their list of recommended educational programs, consult one or more of the college guides, or for graduate study refer to *Peterson's Annual Guide to Graduate Study*. The Guide is an excellent source of detailed information on individual programs. Most college and large public libraries have copies of the Guide.

Before you begin the job search, develop a good résumé or curriculum vitae that summarizes your job qualifications.

Résumés differ from CVs in several respects. The résumé is an informal document intended to indicate one's qualifications for a particular type of position, whereas the CV tends to be a more formal job and academic history, usually several pages in length. The CV is more appropriate for most jobs in hospitals. Résumés are less standardized in format; CVs are developed around defined information usually under specific headings: Personal Data, Educational Background, Work Experience, Professional Affiliations, Honors and Awards, Publications and Presentations.

Develop your CV systematically. It is a good idea to begin with worksheets for each of the headings above. List items under the appropriate headings, rewording and revising until you achieve a satisfactory product. Before finalizing your CV, review it as to overall appearance, layout, relevance of information, conciseness, writing style, completeness, and adequacy in its emphasis on your key accomplishments.

A *cover letter* tailored to the job for which you are applying should accompany your CV. For instance, if you are applying for the directorship of a Patient Representative Department, you would mention specifically your work and volunteer experience in any position that required advocacy functions, membership in relevant professional or community organizations, and any workshops or courses attended that would enhance your skills or knowledge in the field.

Finally, get the most out of every interview.

Think of each interview as an opportunity to learn more about the field and the organization to which you are applying. True, you have been invited for an interview so that the prospective employer can learn more about you and your qualifications. But don't forget its potential as a learning resource to help you focus on the kind of job and work setting that will be best for you. Each interview serves as practice for the next one, and you will be able to observe progress in your interviewing skills as you continue your job search.

A good interview includes the following stages:

Breaking the ice. Establish rapport with some informal conversation, but don't allow small talk to expand this part of the interview.

Sharing of information. This is the time to answer the interviewer's questions (you would do well to anticipate some of the standard ones so that you have ready answers). It is also a time for you to learn about the job and the organization to supplement your preparation in this area prior to the interview. You will be less nervous if you begin to focus on how the information you can get from the interview will help you in the search for a satisfying job.

Sharpening the focus. The goal of this stage is to determine the compatibility between you and the available position. You should be able to contribute substantially to the decision by noting your abilities and achievements in relation to the job that has been discussed in the earlier part of the interview.

Tying it together.   This is the time to clarify information and make closing comments that indicate your enthusiasm for the job. Also, establish what happens next in the recruitment process; i.e., who will call whom and when.

Don't get discouraged. It takes time to find the right kind of job that will lead to an exciting and rewarding career in the hospital.

Glossary

admitting department   Unit in the hospital that handles patient admissions, discharges, and transfers and most of the procedures carried out when patients die.

American Hospital Association (AHA)   Professional association for hospitals and their personnel. The AHA is an educational and informational organization that promotes high standards for hospitals and their employees.

asepsis   Absence of bacteria, fungi, viruses, and other microorganisms that could cause disease; aseptic (adj.)

cardiac catheterization   Introduction of a tube into an artery or vein of the arm or leg so as to manipulate dyes into the chambers of the heart for diagnostic purposes.

cataract   Opacity in the lens of the eye, resulting in blurred vision.

certificate of need statement (CON)   Certificate issued by a governmental body to an individual or an organization proposing to construct or modify a health facility or to offer a new service. CONs are used to help control the expansion of services and facilities beyond demonstrated need.

emphysema   Air in the tissues. In pulmonary emphysema the lungs are enlarged and damaged, reducing the patient's ability to exchange oxygen and carbon dioxide.

epidemiology   Study of the nature, cause, control, and determinants of the frequency and distribution of disease and disability in populations. The epidemiology of a disease is a description of the factors that control the disease's presence or absence in a population.

Health Care Financing Administration (HCFA) Government
agency that establishes procedures for invoking sanctions on
health care providers that furnish services that are not medically
necessary or do not meet designated quality standards. Practitioners may be refused Medicare or Medicaid reimbursement
or be fined for lack of compliance with the regulations.

health maintenance organization (HMO) Organization that em-
ploys or contracts with health care providers to give care to
enrolled members, who agree to prepay for the care through
periodic payments not linked to the quantity of services that
they receive.

health systems agency (HSA) Health planning and resource development agencies created by Public Law 93-641 to perform
specified functions in the service areas designated in the Law.
Functions of the HSAs include the preparation of a Health
Service Plan (HSP) and an Annual Implementation Plan (AIP)
to accomplish priorities established in the Law. HSAs also issue
grants and contracts and review and recommend approval or
disapproval of new services and facilities in their areas to the
state planning agencies.

Hill-Burton Act Legislation enacted in 1946 that provided for
the construction and remodeling of hospitals and other health
care facilities.

infection Invasion of the body by pathogens and the reaction of
the body to the harmful organisms.

Joint Commission on Accreditation of Hospitals (JCAH) Private, nonprofit organization whose function is to encourage the
attainment of uniformly high standards of institutional medical
care. It comprises representatives from the AHA, American
Medical Association, American College of Physicians, and American College of Surgeons. JCAH establishes guidelines for
the operation of hospitals and other health care facilities and
conducts survey and accreditation programs. Accreditation is
granted on the basis of inspection reports written by a staff of
medical inspectors.

Medicare Enacted in 1966 as title XVIII of the Social Security
Act to provide health insurance for persons 65 and over, for
persons eligible for social security disability payments for over

two years, and for certain workers and their dependents who need kidney dialysis or transplantation.

pathogen   Microorganism that causes disease.

Professional Standards Review Organization (PSRO)   Physician-sponsored organization charged with comprehensive and ongoing review of services provided under Medicare, Medicaid, and Maternal and Child Health programs. Purpose is to determine need, quality standards, and appropriate settings for the delivery of care.

Index